Armies of the Germanic Peoples, 200 BC to AD 500

Armies of the Germanic Peoples, 200 BC to AD 500

History, Organization and Equipment

Gabriele Esposito

Pen & Sword
MILITARY

First published in Great Britain in 2021
by Pen & Sword Military
An imprint of Pen & Sword Books Limited
47 Church Street
Barnsley
South Yorkshire
S70 2AS

ISBN 978 1 52677 270 1

A CIP catalogue record for this book is
available from the British Library

Typeset in Adobe Caslon
by Mac Style

Printed and bound in India by Replika Press Pvt. Ltd.

Pen & Sword Books Limited incorporates the imprints of Atlas,
Archaeology, Aviation, Discovery, Family History, Fiction, History, Maritime,
Military, Military Classics, Politics, Select, Transport, True Crime, Air World,
Frontline Publishing, Leo Cooper, Remember When, Seaforth Publishing,
The Praetorian Press, Wharncliffe Local History, Wharncliffe Transport,
Wharncliffe True Crime and White Owl.

For a complete list of Pen & Sword titles please contact
PEN & SWORD BOOKS LIMITED
47 Church Street, Barnsley, South Yorkshire, S70 2AS, England
E-mail: enquiries@pen-and-sword.co.uk
Website: www. pen-and-sword.co.uk

Contents

Acknowledgements   vii
Introduction   viii

Chapter 1   The Early History of the Germani   1

Chapter 2   The Cimbrian War   14

Chapter 3   Julius Caesar and the Germani   37

Chapter 4   The Campaigns of Augustus in Germania   60

Chapter 5   Arminius and the Battle of Teutoburg   74

Chapter 6   The *limes* of the Rhine and the Marcomannic Wars   91

Chapter 7   The Migration Period and the Battle of Adrianople   108

Chapter 8   The Sacks of Rome and the Battle of the Catalaunian Plains 125

Chapter 9   Weapons and Tactics of the Germani   147

Bibliography   165
The Re-enactors who Contributed to this Book   167
Index   168

Gabriele Esposito is a military historian who works as a freelance author and researcher for some of the most important publishing houses in the military history sector. In particular, he is an expert specializing in uniformology: his interests and expertise range from the ancient civilizations to modern post-colonial conflicts. During recent years, he has conducted and published several researches on the military history of the Latin American countries, with special attention on the War of the Triple Alliance and the War of the Pacific. He is among the leading experts on the military history of the Italian Wars of Unification and the Spanish Carlist Wars. His books and essays are published on a regular basis by Osprey Publishing, Winged Hussar Publishing and Libreria Editrice Goriziana; he is also the author of numerous military history articles appearing in specialized magazines like *Ancient Warfare Magazine*, *Medieval Warfare Magazine*, *The Armourer*, *History of War*, *Guerres et Histoire*, *Focus Storia* and *Focus Storia Wars*.

Acknowledgements

This book is dedicated to my fantastic parents, Maria Rosaria and Benedetto, for the great love and precious support that they continue to give me every day. It is thanks to their observations over many years that the present work has been much improved. A very special thanks goes to Philip Sidnell, the commissioning editor of my books for Pen & Sword: his love for history and his passion for publishing are truly fundamental for the success of our publications. Many thanks also to the production manager of this title, Matt Jones, for his great competence and enthusiasm. A special acknowledgement goes to Tony Walton, for the editing of this book with his usual passion and competence, as well as for honouring me with his sincere friendship. A very special mention goes to the brilliant re-enactment group that collaborated with its photos to the creation of this book: without the incredible work of research of its members, the final result of this publication would have not been the same. As a result, I want to express my deep gratitude to the Bulgarian living history association Ancient Thrace and to its charismatic leader, Petar Chapkanov.

Introduction

The main aim of this book is to present an overview of the military history of the Germanic peoples and to describe the weapons and tactics employed by them on the battlefields of Antiquity. Our analysis will start from the very origins of the Germanic communities, and will show the importance that the Celtic civilization had for their development. We will describe the first major encounter between the Germanic tribes and the Romans, by reconstructing the bloody events that saw the Cimbri and Teutones invading the lands of the Roman Republic. Much space will be devoted to the campaigns fought by Julius Caesar on the Rhine frontier against the Germanic communities who tried to settle in Gaul, as well as to a key event in the history of the early Roman Empire: the Battle of Teutoburg. The latter encounter transformed the Rhine into a cultural border between two worlds: the Roman and Germanic civilizations. After this turning point of history, Rome ceased its expansion in continental Europe and entered a new phase of its long military history. We will see how the Germanic tribes soon became a great potential menace for the stability of the Roman Empire, with their frequent raids and violent invasions. With the 'Crisis of the Third Century' and the beginning of the Great Migrations, the borders of Rome started to crumble under the pressure of the Germanic invaders and the political scene of Antiquity changed forever. Our analysis will explain how the Germanic warriors were able to crush the Roman military forces on several occasions, and how they gradually transformed the Roman Army from the inside. Our historical review will end with the fall of the Western Roman Empire and the creation of the new Romano-Germanic kingdoms across Europe. There will be space, however, for a final chapter dedicated to the weaponry and tactics employed by the Germanic warriors during the long period taken into account in this book.

Chapter 1

The Early History of the Germani

Broadly speaking, we know extremely little about the origins and the early history of the Germanic peoples. Most of the information that we have about them comes from later written sources that were produced by the Greeks and Romans. During the opening centuries of their long history, the Germani did not create any written document that could be of help in understanding the origins of their communities. The term 'Germani', which will be used in this text to indicate the individuals belonging to the Germanic peoples, is a Latin one used by Roman writers. Indeed, using the word 'Germans' to identify the ancient inhabitants of present-day Northern Europe is considered incorrect by most contemporary scholars, since it could cause some confusion with the inhabitants of present-day Germany. What we know for sure about the Germani is that they were originally part of the various Indo-European peoples migrating into Europe from Central Asia. These, after settling over most of the continent, gave birth to a series of new civilizations that were the result of the fusion between the local cultures of Europe and the new one 'imported' by the Indo-Europeans. Judging by the archaeological finds related to them and the development of their heirs' civilizations, these Indo-Europeans were extremely warlike and masters in working metals for the production of weapons as well as agricultural tools. The Indo-Europeans produced excellent swords and other weapons made of bronze, giving them a great military superiority over the indigenous populations of Europe, who could not produce such sophisticated objects made of metal. The impact of the Indo-Europeans' arrival in Europe was different according to each geographical region, but the newcomers eventually gained dominance over all the areas that they colonized. The Indo-Europeans settling in Scandinavia, most notably in Denmark and southern Sweden, gave birth to a new culture in those areas of Northern Europe. This started to develop around 1700 BC, initiating a historical period that is commonly known as the Nordic Bronze Age, which, if compared with the Southern Bronze Age of peoples such as the Myceneans, was characterized by a series of peculiarities. First of all, it started much later than the Bronze Age of the southern peoples. In addition, it lasted much longer, since it ended only in 500 BC. In Greece, the Bronze Age came to an end around 1100 BC, more or less six centuries before that in southern Scandinavia. Consequently, there was always a big cultural gap between the civilizations of Northern Europe and those of Southern Europe. While the proto-Germans of Scandinavia entered their Iron Age only around 500 BC, the Greek cities of Southern Europe had by that time already invented philosophy and were fighting against the Persian Empire. To understand why the Greeks and Romans considered the peoples of Northern Europe to be 'barbarians', it is extremely important to bear in mind the existence of this great cultural difference. The differences between the various civilizations were simply the product of the Indo-European migrations' different phases. It would thus be a grievous mistake to consider the proto-Germans as a community of under-developed and isolated northern warriors, as they actually had strong commercial links with the Mediterranean peoples and were able to produce excellent metal objects that were sold on the most important markets of the Ancient World. The territories of Northern Europe inhabited by

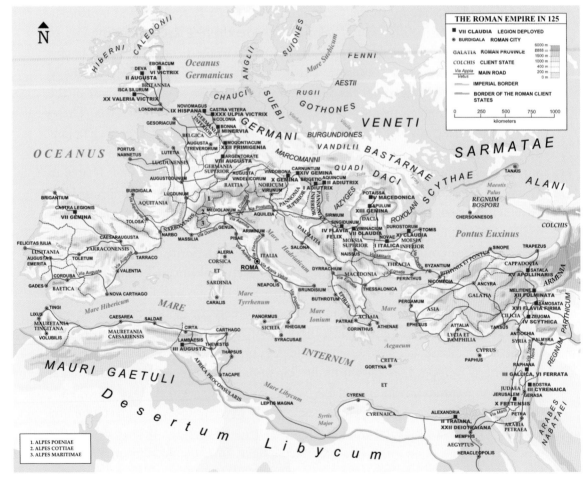

Map of the Roman Empire in AD 125, showing the geographical distribution of the most important Germanic tribes. (*Wikimedia Commons*)

Germanic chieftain with sword and round shield. (*Photo and copyright by Ancient Thrace*)

the proto-Germans were full of strategic natural resources, especially of bronze and copper, which were of vital importance for the production of weapons or agricultural tools and thus were in high demand across the Mediterranean. Over time, the proto-Germans of southern Scandinavia created a commercial route known as the 'Bronze and Copper Road' that connected their territories with the Mycenean world of the south. This crossed most of Europe, from the Baltic Sea to the Black Sea, and was used to transport massive amounts of precious metals or weapons and tools obtained from metals. Thanks to their commercial activities, the proto-Germans improved their economic conditions and started to be influenced (albeit only on a limited scale) by the southern civilizations of the Mediterranean. Together with metals, the proto-Germans also exported large quantities of amber – used in the Ancient World in jewellery and medicine – which could be found only in the areas surrounding the Baltic Sea.

The Nordic Bronze Age was a fundamental phase in the history of the proto-Germans, since it was the moment during which they differentiated themselves from the other Indo-Europeans and acquired many characteristics of the future Germani. The proto-Germans of this period did not live in villages like the contemporary Celts, their settlements consisting instead of isolated farmsteads, with a single 'longhouse' (single-room house) plus some additional minor buildings. Most of the settlements were located on high ground and not far from the Baltic Sea. Agriculture and husbandry were practised, together with fishing in the coastal areas (the remnants of some small canoes have been found), but hunting always remained an important component of the proto-Germans' daily life. At that time, most of Northern Europe was covered with impenetrable forests, inhabited by many wild animals. Living in such an environment was not easy, especially because so little land was available for agriculture and animal husbandry. As a result, horses were not common and only the richest members of each community could afford one. In addition to the 'Bronze and Copper Road', the proto-Germans created a similar and parallel 'Amber Road'; in exchange for metals and amber, they imported precious artefacts to their northern lands, most notably vases. According to archaeological finds, the early religion of the proto-Germans had a lot in common with that of other Indo-European peoples, consisting of a sun-worshipping cult associated with the adoration of various sacred animals such as horses and birds. Similar to the contemporary Celts, the proto-Germans also sacrificed animals and weapons by throwing them into lakes. This ritual practice has preserved (albeit accidentally) many original weapons produced in southern Scandinavia, which have been discovered by archaeologists during the last two centuries.

The Nordic Bronze Age eventually started to be influenced by the southern Hallstatt culture of the Celts, and some of its main features were modified. Around

Germanic warriors living on the Rhine frontier; the figure on the left is armed with a throwing javelin. (*Photo and copyright by Ancient Thrace*)

500 BC, the modifications had solidified, and thus from this date it is possible to speak of a new proto-German culture. This is commonly known as the Jastorf culture, from the name of a village located in Lower Saxony where archaeologists have found many objects related to this new phase in the history of the Germani. Broadly

Germanic warrior equipped with club and hexagonal shield. (*Photo and copyright by Ancient Thrace*)

speaking, the territorial extent of the Jastorf culture was much larger than that of the settlements related to the Nordic Bronze Age, comprising most of northern and central Germany in addition to Denmark and southern Sweden. The Hallstatt culture, which was dominant in southern Germany, was quite different and much more advanced than the culture of the Nordic Bronze Age. Hallstatt is a small village located in the mountains of Austria, near Salzburg, which has become famous due to the rich Celtic burials that were found on its territory (in the proximity of a lake) during the nineteenth century. The name of the village, like many other important archaeological sites in Europe, contains the term 'halle', which usually related to the presence of salt in its territory. Salt was the equivalent of gold during the Bronze Age, and even before, playing a key role in commerce and trade. As a result, possessing a salt mine could determine the fortunes of a community. Salt was a major source of wealth and a fundamental element in the daily life of the time: it was precious enough to be traded for other goods (for example, metal weapons) and was universally used to preserve food. The Celts of southern Germany paid for the metals and amber bought from the proto-Germans mostly with salt. The early Celtic communities of Austria grew rich thanks to the salt trade and soon started to expand their political influence towards bordering territories. Within a few decades, their area of control reached the Rhine on the frontier of France and the Danube on the western border of modern Hungary. During these early centuries, however, Austria and Switzerland remained the core of the Celtic territories. The Alps were rich in mineral resources which the Celts needed in order to maintain their commercial supremacy over other peoples. Consequently, the Celts never expanded north towards the lands of the proto-Germans, but their more advanced culture was partially adopted by the communities of northern Germany and southern Scandinavia. The Jastorf culture and the Hallstatt culture had two main elements in common: the practice of cremation for burials and the production of sophisticated weapons and working tools made from metal.

Around 500 BC, while Greece was at war with the Persian Empire and Rome was struggling to become a Republic after having been ruled by kings, the Celts of Central Europe started to develop a new 'culture' that would correspond to the second and most important phase of their history. This is commonly known as La Tène culture: as with the Hallstatt culture, its name derives from the main archaeological site where important remnants of it were found. 'La Tène' meant 'shallow waters' in the Celtic language, and the site bearing this name is located on the north side of Lake Neuchatel in Switzerland. This place surely had an important religious meaning for the Celts, because it was a site where they made rich offerings to the gods in the form of weapons and other objects that were deposited in a lake. The site was first discovered in 1857 when the water level of the lake dropped, but most of the objects were collected during the period 1906–1917. Thanks to these numerous findings, it has been possible to understand the differences between this new culture and the previous Hallstatt one. First of all, the Celts of La Tène had different burial rites from their ancestors: nobles were buried in light two-wheeled chariots rather than heavy four-wheeled wagons. In addition, the various objects from this new phase of Celtic history show a completely different artistic style. The art of the Hallstatt culture had been characterized by static and mostly geometric decorations, while the new La Tène culture featured many movement-based forms. Most of the weapons and other objects were now decorated with inscribed and inlaid interlace or spirals. The famous neck rings known as 'torques' and the elegant brooches known as 'fibulae' started to be produced on a massive scale during this period, becoming objects of universal use in the Celtic world. Stylized and curvilinear forms, representing sacred animals or plant elements, started to be reproduced on many artefacts. Celtic art was no longer based on abstract motifs, but tried to reproduce the natural world from a religious point of view. As is stressed by many scholars of the period, the La Tène culture was the result of the continuous cultural and commercial contacts that the Celts had with the Mediterranean world: Greek, Etruscan and Roman influences all contributed to the development of this new phase of Celtic civilization.

The new La Tène culture influenced the Germani like the previous Hallstatt culture, but its diffusion in central and northern Germany was very slow, taking place only around 400 bc, one century later than its early development in the Celtic world. The Jastorf culture of the proto-Germans lasted from 500 bc to ad 10, and it was during this long period, around 120 bc, that the proto-Germans first came into close contact with the southern peoples of the Mediterranean. This event was fundamental for the development of their identity and marked the transformation of the proto-Germans into Germani. The key event in this historical process was the Cimbrian War, which saw the migration of two major Germanic tribes towards the lands dominated by the Roman Republic. It should be noted, however, that some communities of Germani had already been in contact with the Mediterranean world well before that date. During the period from 500–400 bc, the Jastorf culture was mostly influenced by the Hallstatt culture, which was already on the verge of disappearing from the Celtic world. From 400 bc, it came under the influence of the La Tène culture and gradually started to develop some more peculiar features. These were partly the result of the first mass migrations involving the Germani. The first Germanic tribe to move towards Southern Europe was that of the Bastarnae. These were a large tribe of mixed Celtic-Germanic descent, which originally settled in present-day Moldavia before moving south towards the heart of the Balkans around 200 bc. In 179 bc, the Bastarnae crossed the Danube in great numbers, having been

Frankish warrior with light javelin and hexagonal shield. (*Photo and copyright by Ancient Thrace*)

Germanic chieftain equipped with sword and round shield. (*Photo and copyright by Ancient Thrace*)

invited to do so by Philip V, King of Macedonia. Philip V had recently been defeated by the Romans during the Second Macedonian War, and had been obliged by the victors to severely reduce the size of his armed forces. This caused serious problems to Macedonia because the new army was too small to effectively defend the eastern borders of the realm from the regular attacks of the Illyrian and Thracian tribes.

To resolve this issue, Philip V intended to settle the Bastarnae on his eastern frontier as 'military colonists': they would provide the defence of the area from enemy raids and be loyal subjects of the Macedonians. In addition, in case of a new war against Rome (which seemed very probable), they could be employed as a significant part of the Macedonian Army. The Bastarnae accepted Philip V's offer and started to migrate south, but while on the march, they learned that the Macedonian king had died and that they were no longer expected in their new homeland. At this point they decided to raid and pillage the region in which they had stopped, which was Thrace. Hostilities between the Bastarnae and the Thracians were particularly violent. The Bastarnae besieged various Thracian strongholds but without success, and were later ambushed on several occasions by the Thracian warriors. At this point, half of the Bastarnae decided to return north to their homeland, while the remainder (amounting to some 30,000 people) remained on the eastern frontier of Macedonia. Philip V's successor, Perseus, allowed the Bastarnae to settle on the territory of the Illyrian and Thracian tribes that attacked Macedonia's eastern frontier. These tribes assaulted the winter camp that had been built by the Bastarnae, but were repulsed with heavy losses. The conflict continued with an offensive by the Bastarnae against their enemies, but this ended in failure when the Celtic-Germanic warriors were crushed during an ambush. The Bastarnae had little knowledge of their new homeland, and thus were greatly exposed to ambushes when moving in large numbers, while during pitched battles, they were no match for any possible enemy. Having lost their entire baggage and supplies during the ambush, they had no choice but to return home to Moldavia. Many of them then died while crossing the frozen Danube on foot, and others were killed when attacked by the local tribes. Several decades after these events, the Bastarnae were gradually able to recover from the losses suffered during their failed migration. They then found themselves at war with the expanding Dacian kingdom of King Burebista, who wanted to unify all the peoples living along the eastern part of the Danube under his personal rule and to attack the Romans in Macedonia in order to expel them from the region. To do this, he wanted to obtain the decisive military support of the Bastarnae, who were considered the best warriors in the Balkans by most contemporary observers. Hostilities between the Dacians and the Bastarnae did not last for long, ending up with the victory of Burebista. The Celtic-Germanic warriors then became allies of the Dacians and contributed to the further enlargement of Burebista's army.

Germanic slinger using his weapon. (*Photo and copyright by Ancient Thrace*)

Goth warrior with spear and round shield. (*Photo and copyright by Ancient Thrace*)

Chapter 2

The Cimbrian War

Around 150 BC there was a demographic explosion in southern Scandinavia. This caused a rapid expansion of the local population that was not sustainable for the natural environment of Northern Europe. As a result, two of the most important Germanic tribes settled in the Jutland Peninsula decided to migrate south in search of new lands to inhabit. These tribes were the Cimbri and Teutones. During the previous decades, the Germanic communities had intensified their commercial exchanges with the Celts, from which they had learned something about the rich southern lands that were dominated by the Romans. These regions around the Mediterranean were sunny and perfect for agriculture, and furthermore were characterized by the presence of important natural resources and the existence of large urban centres inhabited by thousands of citizens. These southern lands would have been a perfect new homeland for the Germani, who could no longer survive in Northern Europe due to a terrible lack of food. Having no other choice and being confident that their future would be a flourishing one, the warlike Cimbri and Teutones moved south and crossed Germany in search of new lands. They migrated with their families and all their goods: they were 'peoples on the move', a Germanic tradition that would continue well after the fall of the Roman Empire. This early mass migration was unthinkable by the standards of the time, especially to the Romans. Many thousands of warriors and their families were pushing towards the northern frontier of the Roman Republic, with carts full of goods and hopes for a better life. The Romans, having never experienced anything similar, were not ready to face such a situation. By that time, around 120 BC, Rome already dominated most of the Mediterranean: in Europe alone, it controlled most of Iberia (present-day Spain) and the southern Balkans, in addition to the Italian Peninsula. A few years before the arrival of the Cimbri and Teutones, the Romans had also conquered a large portion of southern Gaul (present-day France). This region had been crossed by Hannibal with his Carthaginian army during the Second Punic War, so the Romans wanted a buffer zone on the north-western border of the Italian Peninsula in order to prevent any future invasion of Italy coming from Gaul. This area was still inhabited by Celts, like the rest of Gaul, but was organized as a Roman province (hence its modern name of Provence).

Germanic warrior with winter dress. (*Photo and copyright by Ancient Thrace*)

Goth warrior equipped with spear and round shield. (*Photo and copyright by Ancient Thrace*)

On the north-eastern frontier of the Italian Peninsula, bordering with present-day Austria, the Romans had organized another buffer zone for protection of the Republic. This did not consist of a province, but a client state known as the Kingdom of Noricum. This was originally inhabited by several Celtic tribes, which were gradually unified into a 'federal state' that was under the strong influence of Rome. The Celts of Noricum had strong political and commercial relations with those living in Pannonia (Hungary) and the other Celtic tribes settled in Switzerland. Noricum was in a delicate geographical position, with Roman Italy to the south and the fierce Germanic 'nations' to the north. As a result, its political leaders had no choice but to form an alliance with the Roman Republic in order to obtain their military protection. The Kingdom of Noricum was created around 150 BC, and from the beginning it provided the Romans with large amounts of excellent weapons. Celtic Austria was famous for the high-quality production of metal weapons and tools. Noricum was rich in iron, gold and salt, natural resources that both the Romans and the Germani badly needed, and thus the local Celts had to maintain some kind of equilibrium in order to preserve their independence. Noric steel was particularly appreciated for its quality and hardness: most of the weapons used to equip the Roman legions were obtained from it. Between Provence and Noricum, in present-day Switzerland, the political situation was quite different, as the local Celts did not have positive relations with Rome. By the second century BC, the Swiss plateau was entirely occupied by the Helvetii, who lived on territory that was full of natural resources, especially of gold (which was widely found in rivers as well as being mined). The Helvetii were not a single tribe, but a confederation of four tribes; apparently they originally lived in southern Germany, but around 150 BC, under strong pressure from the Germanic tribes of the north, they had to move south and settle in the Alpine area. It is often assumed that both the confederation of the Helvetii and the Kingdom of Noricum were formed around the middle of the second century BC as a result of the Germanic mass-migrations of the Cimbri and Teutones.

Before reaching the Danube, and thus the Kingdom of Noricum, the Cimbri and Teutones encountered and defeated the tribe of the Scordisci during their march. The latter were a Celtic tribe originally settled in modern Hungary, which had participated in the great Celtic 'invasion' of the Balkans that saw the sacking of Greece. During their march home after the end of the expedition, the Scordisci decided to stop at the mouth of the River Sava and to build new settlements there. Philip V of Macedonia developed a very good relationship with them, since he wanted to use these Celts as allies against the Illyrian and Thracian tribes as well as Rome (exactly like the Bastarnae). The Scordisci soon became a significant regional power of the central Balkans: they built two fortresses to protect their new territory and submitted several of the local tribes. After the transformation of Macedonia into a Roman province in 146 BC, they were constantly at war against the Romans and launched frequent incursions of their territory. In 135 BC, the Romans obtained their first victory over the Scordisci, part of whom then moved north, settling on the eastern borders of Noricum and Pannonia. These refugees were crushed by the Germani coming from the north, and most of their surviving members had no choice but to join the Cimbri and Teutones in their attack on Noricum. The Taurisci were the first Celtic tribe of Norocum to be invested by the newcomers, who were incredibly powerful militarily. The warriors of the Cimbri and Teutones were ferocious and wild by the Celtic and Roman standards of the time, showing no fear in battle and being prone to launching devastating frontal assaults. Having nothing to lose, their only chance of survival was the possibility of finding new lands to settle. Consequently, they used all their energies to defeat the enemies they encountered on their way. They came from an ancestral world that was completely different from that of the Celts and the Romans: they were used to surviving for many days with little food and had no idea what a city was. For their entire life, the warriors of the Cimbri and Teutones had lived in cold forests and had always been fighting for their own survival. They were thus tough fighters, who did not show any respect for the military superiority of the Romans and used field tactics that had never before been seen by the legions.

In 112 BC, the Roman Republic sent a large army to the Kingdom of Noricum, under the command of the consul Gnaeus Papirius Carbo, who was ordered to make an impressive show of force against the migrating tribes in order to convince them that an invasion of Noricum was not practicable. Initially, the Germani tried to negotiate with the Romans and asked for some lands to settle, but it soon became clear that the legions had not crossed the Alps only to make a demonstration. As a result, the first ever battle between Germani and Romans was fought at Noreia, on the eastern borders of Noricum. This ended in complete disaster for the Roman legions and their Celtic allies, with the Cimbri and Teutones able to crush most of the forces that had been sent against them. Carbo escaped with his life only with great difficulty, and the Roman army that had been sent north was practically destroyed. The Romans had been taken by surprise, but had now learned that the Germani were completely different from all the other peoples that they had encountered in battle. The determination and courage of the Germani were unrivalled in the Ancient World, even if their warriors had very simple personal equipment that did not include armour like that used by the Romans and Celts. The legionaries were shocked by the fighting methods of these 'primitives' from the north, and the psychological element represented by fear played a significant part in the early defeats suffered by the Romans at the hands of the Germani. The Roman Senate

Goth warrior. (*Photo and copyright by Ancient Thrace*)

Germanic chieftain inciting his warriors. (*Photo and copyright by Ancient Thrace*)

punished Carbo for his defeat, removing him from his position as consul and causing his subsequent suicide. The Italian Peninsula now lay open to invasion by the Cimbri and Teutones, since the Alps had been crossed by the Germani and no other Roman troops remained between them and the heart of Italy. Just when it seemed that a new sack of Rome was imminent, events took an unexpected twist: the Cimbri and the Teutones did not move south towards Italy, as expected and feared, but turned west. They crossed Switzerland and crushed the Helvetii; one of the tribes making up the latter confederation, that of the Tigurini, joined the Germani in their migration and moved with them towards Gaul.

In 109 BC, the Cimbri and the Teutones devastated most of Roman Provence, after having defeated the local military forces of Rome. These events led to the creation of a stable and formal alliance between the Germani and the Celtic Tigurini, which created an extremely dangerous situation for the Romans. In just a few years, the Cimbri and Teutones had completely destroyed the network of alliances that Rome had created around the Alps for the protection of Italy: the Kingdom of Noricum had been invaded and sacked, part of the Helvetii had joined the Germani and Roman Provence had been completely ravaged. In 107 BC, the Senate sent a new army against the Germani, attacking a large camp that had been built by the latter at Burdigala (present-day Bordeaux). However, the Roman legions were ambushed by the Germani before they could even reach the enemy positions and were massacred: some 10,000 Romans were killed in the clash and all the supplies of the new army assembled by the Senate had to be left behind. After such a crushing defeat, most of the recently conquered Celtic communities of southern France rose up in revolt against Rome and joined the invaders. In 106 BC, the Romans sent another army to southern Gaul, which obtained some minor victories over the rebellious Celts. During the following year, however, a larger and much more decisive battle was fought between the legions and the Germani at Arausio. The Romans attacked the new large encampment that had been built by the Cimbri with the intention of killing as many of the Germani as possible, but the assault was repulsed with very high casualties and this battle ended in another massacre for the Roman forces. After crushing the legions, the Cimbri assaulted the Roman camp (which was left practically undefended) and plundered it. The defeat at Arausio was particularly alarming for the Romans, since the Germani had been able to crush a Roman military force of over 80,000 soldiers. The Alpine passes were now again left undefended, and the high casualties suffered produced a serious lack of manpower for the Roman Army. Apart from the Battle of Cannae that took place during the Second Punic War, Arausio was the worst defeat ever suffered by a Roman army up to this time. The Cimbri and Teutones had proved themselves to be the most dangerous enemy faced by the Senate since Hannibal. However, once again the Germani did not attempt an invasion of Italy at this time: strangely, they decided to move further west and occupy Iberia. The north-western part of Iberia was inhabited by several independent Celtiberian tribes, with the Romans controlling the south-eastern portion of the peninsula. It is not known why the Germani, for a second time, chose not to invade Italy, although it is likely that they did not know that the Romans had no more troops and did not have a clear knowledge of the territories on which they were moving. Whatever the case, the decision taken after the Battle of Arausio was a negative one for them. It is important to note, however, that only the Cimbri invaded Iberia, while the Teutones preferred to remain in southern Gaul.

The Celtiberians were much more warlike than the other Celtic communities that the Cimbri had encountered during their migration. They were the result of an 'ethnic mix' that took place between the Iberians and the Celts who settled in Spain, and thus had some peculiar features that were not found among the Celtic inhabitants of Gaul. The Celtiberians had been at war with Rome for decades in order to preserve their independence, and had been a fundamental component of Hannibal's Carthaginian army. They were skilled horsemen and knew how to fight in the mountains of their homeland by using hit-and-run tactics. Thanks to such tactics, they had been able to defend their autonomy and had defeated the Romans on several occasions. When the Cimbri invaded Iberia, the Celtiberian tribes formed a strong military alliance and moved against them. We know very little of the war that was fought between the Cimbri and the Celtiberians, only that the latter were able to defeat the invaders (probably through ambush) and forced them to return to southern Gaul. The Cimbri were probably surprised by the fighting capabilities of the Celtiberians, as they had been able to defeat several other Celtic communities quite easily in previous clashes. The time spent by the Germani in Iberia was taken advantage of by the Romans to reorganize their military forces and the defences of Italy. After the Battle of Arausio, the *terror cimbricus* (the 'fear of the Cimbri') was spreading in the Italian Peninsula, and the Senate feared that Rome could be destroyed by the wild Germani.

At this time, the Roman Army was experiencing many difficulties and needed to be completely reformed. Until the Second Punic War, Roman armies had been made up of citizen-soldiers who became conscripts only for a limited period of time (usually corresponding to the duration of a military campaign) and who returned to their regular civil life as soon as their services were no longer needed. In addition, the various citizen-soldiers had different personal equipment and tactical roles according to their *census*, i.e. their economic capabilities. During the Second Punic War, this kind of military system had shown all its limits, since the campaigns that were fought

Germanic skirmisher equipped with javelins and small rectangular shield. (*Photo and copyright by Ancient Thrace*)

Goth warrior. (*Photo and copyright by Ancient Thrace*)

against Hannibal lasted for many years. Being unable to return home after just a few months of military service, the citizen-soldiers could not work on their farms as they had always done, and this caused great damage to the economy of the Roman Republic. Without the necessary manpower, Roman agriculture could not sustain prolonged war efforts. In addition, the Romans often had to send expeditionary corps to Iberia and Africa during the Second Punic War in order to fight against the Carthaginians who dominated those territories. This meant that thousands of Italic soldiers had to leave their home territory for months or even years, being obliged to serve as professional soldiers rather than as temporary recruits. During the great military emergency that followed the Battle of Cannae, Rome was obliged to recruit thousands of *proletarii* in order to replenish the losses suffered at the hands of the Carthaginians. The *proletarii* were the poorest citizens of Roman society, individuals who had never been part of the military system because they were too poor to equip

Germanic warrior armed with club and short scramasax sword. (*Photo and copyright by Ancient Thrace*)

Germanic warrior equipped with long club. (*Photo and copyright by Ancient Thrace*)

themselves properly (their only personal possession was the *prole*, i.e. numerous sons and daughters). To face the menace represented by Hannibal, the Roman Republic gave the necessary personal equipment to thousands of poor citizens and admitted them into the ranks of the legions. When the Carthaginians were finally defeated, the Roman Army continued to recruit *proletarii* and gradually started to modify its organization.

After the Battle of Arausio, it became apparent to those in power at Rome that a major military reform had to be carried out, and this was done by Gaius Marius. One of Rome's greatest generals and a man of great experience, Marius had already fought at the head of an army on several occasions. Marius decided to transform the Roman Army into a force made up of professional soldiers from the poorest social groups of the Republic: these would serve in the army for most of their life and be equipped by the state. The era of the citizen-soldier was over: the new professional legionaries would earn a living thanks to their military career and would be available to serve in every corner of the Mediterranean, with no time limits. Marius greatly improved the training and discipline of Rome's military forces, giving to each legionary heavy personal equipment that included several working tools: each soldier would therefore be able to operate as a 'combat engineer' if needed, to build fortified encampments or destroy the fortifications of the enemy. Due to their new and much heavier equipment, the professional soldiers of the reformed Roman Army soon became known as the 'mules of Marius'. The reform that followed the Battle of Arausio also affected the tactics of the Roman Army, since Gaius Marius decided to abolish the differentiation existing in the weaponry carried by the legionaries: they were no longer divided into separate categories but all received the same panoply, with chainmail and oval shield. Finally, the previous tactical organization with *manipuli* was replaced by a new one based on *cohortes*, which were stronger than the *manipuli* because they comprised a higher number of men and thus were well suited to face the massive frontal charges of the Germani. Using the *terror cimbricus* to his advantage, Marius infringed the Roman constitution by being elected consul for several years without interruption. In the eyes of the majority of the Romans, he was the only man who could save the Republic from desperation and destruction. The ambitious consul did his best to transform the Roman Army into his own private force, by creating strong personal links with his officers and creating a new *esprit de corps* inside the legions. He was the first, for example, to give a distinctive standard and a peculiar denomination to each unit of the Roman Army. After completing his reforms and the training of his new armed forces, Gaius Marius moved against the Cimbri and Teutones at the head of his renewed army.

In 102 BC, after the failure of their Iberian campaign, the Cimbri returned to southern Gaul and joined their forces with those of the Teutones who had remained there. At this point they decided to move south towards Italy, since it became clear that they could not remain in Gaul. The local Celtic communities, after some initial enthusiasm for the Germani's arrival, had changed their attitude and were now organizing themselves to expel them. The powerful Arverni, in particular, had already attacked the Teutones and had no intention of accepting the presence of foreigners on the borders of their homeland. Marching through the region of Savoy, the Germani entered northern Italy with a two-pronged movement: the Teutones, in the west, invaded the Italian peninsula by marching along the coastal road that connected southern Gaul with Liguria; the Cimbri, in the east, crossed the Julian and Carnic Alps to attack Piedmont from the north. Gaius Marius, considering that the Teutones would reach the plains of northern Italy before the Cimbri – who had to cross the Alps – decided to move with all his forces against them. He did not attack at first, but waited to see the moves of the enemy. The Teutones tried to provoke the Romans into fighting a large pitched battle, but Marius continued to be very

Goth warrior with spear and shield. (*Photo and copyright by Ancient Thrace*)

Germanic warrior with sword and round shield. (*Photo and copyright by Ancient Thrace*)

prudent and gathered his forces into a large fortified camp. This camp was assaulted by the Germani, who were very impatient to defeat the Romans, but their attack was easily repulsed by the Romans because the Teutones did not have any experience of storming prepared fortifications. Unwilling to attempt another attack against the Roman positions, the Germani marched past Marius' camp and moved on towards Italy. It took a staggering six days for all the Teutones to move from their original positions, their movements being slowed because they had their families and wagons with them. Marius did not attack the Germani while they were on the move, since he was in search of the perfect location where he could organize an ambush. During the following days, the Romans followed them cautiously and closely, maintaining a judicious distance from them and fighting several skirmishes with the rearguard of the Germani.

The Teutones eventually decided to stop and face the Romans at Aquae Sextie, near modern Aix-en-Provence. The location of the upcoming battle had been chosen well by the Germani, since it consisted of a large plain on which they could deploy their superior numbers and launch a series of devastating frontal assaults. The Teutones, however, made a serious tactical mistake before the arrival of the Romans, failing to occupy some higher ground that dominated the battlefield. Marius, upon reaching the battlefield, swiftly occupied this high ground and gave precise orders to his legionaries: they were to wait for the frontal assault of the Teutones, throw their javelins from the hill against the advancing Germani, then draw their short swords and push the enemy back from the high ground. By doing so, Marius was using the morphology of the terrain to his advantage: the Teutones would only have reached the Roman positions on the top of the hill after a lengthy charge conducted under a rain of javelins and on broken terrain. Charging uphill in these conditions would have been extremely difficult, even for some warriors like the Germani. Everything went as planned by the Roman commander: the Teutones charged uphill but were decimated by the Roman javelins during their advance. The survivors who reached the top had to face a compact mass of legionaries, who were perfectly disciplined and ready to stop the *furor* ('fury') of the attackers. Despite their great courage and determination, the Teutones were unable to dislodge the Romans from their strong positions and were pushed back downhill after suffering severe losses. After several hours of combat, the battle had moved to the plain that was located at the centre of the battlefield, with the Germani initially holding their ground against the Romans. However, a chosen force of 3,000 legionaries was sent by Marius to attack the Germani from the rear. Now under strong pressure from two sides, the Teutones quickly broke ranks and started to flee. This was the decisive moment of the battle, the Romans then relentlessly pursuing the defeated Teutones and slaughtering many of them. By the end of the battle, most of the Germani warriors had been killed and all their families had been captured.

After the Battle of Aquae Sextie, the Teutones ceased to be a menace for Rome. More than 100,000 Germani had been killed or captured, including many women and children who were sold as slaves on the Roman markets. Teutobod, the leader of the Teutones, was able to escape from the battlefield with some 3,000 warriors, although these were soon captured by the Celtic tribe of the Sequani. These allies of the Roman Republic handed over the captured Germani to Marius. After obtaining such a brilliant victory, the Roman general mustered his remaining 37,000 men and marched against the Cimbri, who were moving south. By July of 101 BC, the Germani were heading westwards along the banks of the River Po, the main waterway of northern Italy which crossed the most fertile plains of the peninsula. The Romans deployed south of the Po in a strong defensive position, but initially Marius tried to negotiate with the Germani instead of attacking them. The Roman general attempted to demoralize the Cimbri by parading in front of them the captured nobles of the Teutones. However, neither side had the intention of conducting serious negotiations: the Romans merely needed to gain time in order to organize their forces, while the Cimbri had no choice but to move south in order to survive. Marius chose a perfect location for the ensuing battle, consisting of an open plain known as the Raudine Plain (near present-day Vercellae). In total, Marius now commanded an army of 52,000 soldiers, while the Cimbri could deploy a total of 120,000 warriors. After completing their preparations, the Romans moved north of the Po and offered battle to the enemy. Marius divided his forces into three groups: two wings, each with 16,000 legionaries, which were made up of veteran soldiers who had already fought against the Teutones, and a centre with 20,000 new recruits with little military experience. The Romans deployed first on the battlefield and thus obliged the Cimbri to fight with the sun in their eyes. On the day of the battle, the wind was blowing towards the Germani, who thus had to contend with a further disadvantage. According to ancient sources, the Cimbri had a strong cavalry contingent of 15,000 horsemen that was deployed in front of their infantry; the latter consisted of more than 100,000 warriors, who were assembled into an enormous square-shaped formation.

The Cimbri attacked first, the Romans having not moved from their positions when the enemy warriors appeared on the battlefield. While the Germani were advancing towards the Romans, Marius launched a rapid attack with his left wing against the right of the Cimbri. The Germani, however, countered this move by developing their forces into an enormous wedge formation that had the cavalry at the front. The Germani attacked with violence and determination, investing the centre of the Roman army, but despite their efforts, they were not able to break the enemy lines

Frankish warrior. (*Photo and copyright by Ancient Thrace*)

Frankish warrior equipped with sword and round shield. (*Photo and copyright by Ancient Thrace*)

and suffered very high casualties. Meanwhile, the cavalry of the Cimbri attacked the Roman right but were quickly repulsed and routed by the superior mounted forces of Marius. The defeated cavalrymen of the Germani were pushed back towards the ranks of their infantry, which caused great confusion among the Cimbri, who were not able to keep order in their ranks. Then, at the key moment of the battle, the Roman right and centre advanced against the disordered Cimbri, killing many of them. The ensuing hand-to-hand fighting was terrible: the legionaries pushed forward against the Cimbri and pressed them into an ever-reducing space. The Germani thus could not move freely and use their long slashing swords, while the Romans could easily employ their shorts swords to slaughter their opponents. Marius, with the left wing that was under his direct command, returned to the battlefield after having searched in vain for the Cimbri on the right, and attacked the Germani from the rear. The Cimbri were by now completely surrounded by the Romans, and the battle developed into a massacre. Sapped of energy by the hard fighting and summer heat, the Germani, now with no hope of victory, could only surrender or be killed. Some surviving Cimbri retreated to the wagons that made up the rearguard of their army, where they attempted a last stand with the support of their women and children. However, the Romans continued their advance and massacred all the Germani,

Germanic warrior with rectangular shield. (*Photo and copyright by Ancient Thrace*)

Germanic chieftain of the Suebi. (*Photo and copyright by Ancient Thrace*)

including their leader Boiorix. All the women and children who were not killed by the legionaries, or who did not commit suicide, were captured and later sold as slaves.

With the Battle of Vercellae, the threat posed by the Cimbri to the Roman Republic was also eradicated, and the Cimbrian War thereby came to an end. The war is of particular importance from a historical point of view because it saw the first encounter between two extremely different civilizations: the northern Germani and the southern Romans. Rome had initially been taken by complete surprise by the fighting methods and determination of the northern warriors, but after the disaster of Arausio and the subsequent ascendancy of Gaius Marius, the Romans were able to recover. From a military point of view, the Cimbrian War was a real turning point in the history of the Roman Army: the Romans had transformed their fighting forces into a professional organization that was made up of volunteers serving as soldiers for most of their life. The new standard panoply and the new organization on *cohortes* introduced by Marius remained unchanged until the third century AD, thus becoming fundamental components of Roman warfare. For the Germani, the lessons learned during the attempted invasion of Roman territory were very harsh: they had encountered the military power of the legions for the first time and had learned that a better-organized army could defeat them on the open field. Both the Cimbri and the Teutones were completely annihilated by the Romans, since their entire population was either killed or captured. News of their 'adventure' in Southern Europe soon spread in their home territories, and no other tribes mounted attacks against the lands of the Roman Republic during the following decades. After defeating the Germani, the Romans entered into a new phase of their long history that was characterized by the outbreak of civil wars. The first of these saw Marius on one side and Sulla on the other, with the winning general of the Cimbrian War facing a young officer who had commanded the Roman cavalry at the Battle of Vercellae. The Romans only encountered the Germani again several decades after the end of the Cimbrian War, when Julius Caesar launched his bloody conquest of Gaul. The events of 113–101 BC, as we will see, were just the first round in a terrible clash of civilizations that would last for centuries. Thanks to their early experiences of the Cimbrian War, both the Germani and the Romans learned a lot about their enemies and could prepare themselves for future campaigns.

Chapter 3

Julius Caesar and the Germani

Gaul, the core of the Celtic civilization, was conquered by Rome in a very short time if compared with Iberia. Unlike what happened in Spain, the Celts living in present-day France had to face an incredibly effective Roman commander: Julius Caesar. He started to rule Rome jointly with Crassus and Pompey from 60 BC, when the three formed the famous First Triumvirate. In 58 BC, after being consul in Rome for one year, Julius Caesar obtained the proconsulship of Cisalpine Gaul (northern Italy) and Transalpine Gaul (southern France). The great general and future absolute ruler of the Roman Republic badly needed a major military victory in order to consolidate his power and limit the ascendancy of his two colleagues/ rivals. Crassus was the richest man in Rome and had already obtained a great military triumph in ending the slave revolt of Spartacus, while Pompey had conducted and won many brilliant campaigns against some of Rome's fiercest enemies. Caesar was ambitious and had great personal capabilities, but unlike the other members of the Triumvirate he had never been at the head of a large army. Obtaining command over the troops of the two Gauls was a great opportunity for him, as these provinces were 'border' areas at the time, where a young and intelligent general could learn a lot by fighting against local enemies. The vast Celtic lands of central and northern Gaul were ripe for the picking by Caesar and his legions. The Roman leader knew full well that by conquering Gaul, the Roman Republic would become the greatest power in the known world. Indeed, with the natural resources and population of Gaul at their disposal, the Romans could go on to conquer the rest of Europe. Caesar had four veteran legions at his command and was ready to start his campaign of conquest: he only needed a *casus belli* to justify the outbreak of hostilities in the eyes of the Senate. This was given him by the Helvetii, who were experiencing increasing pressure from the Germanic tribes living on their northern borders and were planning to migrate across Roman territory in search of a new home.

The Helvetii wanted to settle on the Atlantic coast of central Gaul and hoped to do so without having to fight during their journey. However, to reach their objective, they had to cross Roman Provence and the territories of the Aedui (another Celtic tribe, the most important ally of the Romans among the Gauls). Caesar was extremely cunning in using this situation to his advantage, presenting the migration of the

Germanic chieftain; note the decorated blade of the scramasax. (*Photo and copyright by Ancient Thrace*)

Germanic warrior of the Suebi. (*Photo and copyright by Ancient Thrace*)

Helvetii as an 'invasion' in order to force the Senate's hand and obtain permission to face this menace with his army. When the Helvetii started their march, only one of Caesar's four legions was stationed in Transalpine Gaul. In no condition to mount an offensive, he initially tried to gain some time by having peace talks with the emissaries of the Helvetii. The latter wanted to negotiate a safe and peaceful passage across Roman territories, having no intention of raiding or pillaging the areas that they were going to traverse. After holding discussions for two weeks, during which he fortified his positions and levied more troops, Caesar rejected all the requests of the Celtic emissaries. At this point the Helvetii tried to enter Roman territory, but were easily thwarted by the new defences organized by Caesar. Meanwhile, Caesar went to Cisalpine Gaul to raise two new legions and bring all his military forces north of the Alps. Understanding that they were now going to face Caesar's whole military force, the Helvetii initiated negotiations with the local tribes of the Sequani and Aedui to form a military alliance against Rome. The Sequani allowed the Helvetii to cross their lands without meeting opposition, whereas the Aedui remained loyal to Rome but saw their territory devastated by the migrating Helvetii. Responding to the Aedui's request for help, Caesar attacked the Helvetii with three legions while they were crossing the River Arar. When the Romans arrived, three of the four Helvetian tribes had already crossed the river, so Caesar was able to destroy only the remaining one. The Roman general, however, continued his close pursuit with great determination. During the ensuing Battle of Bibracte, fought in 58 BC, the Roman legions were finally able to crush the Helvetii, who suffered enormous losses. Their few survivors then surrendered to Caesar.

The Roman victory over the Helvetii, however, did not end hostilities in Gaul, with the Sequani and Aedui continuing to fight each other after their territories were freed from the Helvetii. These two tribes, probably the strongest ones in Gaul at the time, had been at war for a long time and were divided by a very deep rivalry. The Aedui had largely become loyal allies of Rome due to their frequent wars with the Sequani, since they needed a powerful ally to prevail in their long-running dispute. In 63 BC, however, the Sequani had also found a strong ally in the Germanic tribe of the Suebi. Guided by their great warlord Ariovistus, the Suebi had united their forces with those of the Sequani in exchange for some lands in Gaul. At the Battle of Magetobriga in 63 BC, an alliance formed by the Sequani, Arverni and Suebi had soundly defeated the Aedui. This event had caused much apprehension in Rome, where the memories of the devastations caused by the Cimbri and the Teutones were still fresh. The presence of the Suebi in Gaul was considered a real menace, so the Republic decided it must break the alliance between Ariovistus and the various Celtic tribes. After the completion of the joint military operations against the Helvetii,

Goth warrior with sword and round shield. (*Photo and copyright by Ancient Thrace*)

Germanic slinger. (*Photo and copyright by Ancient Thrace*)

the leaders of the Aedui alerted Julius Caesar to their concerns about Ariovistus' expansionism. The Aedui formally requested Roman military help to defeat the Suebi and their Celtic allies: this was the occasion that Caesar had been waiting for to continue his campaigns in Gaul. The Roman general sent an ultimatum to Ariovistus, warning him that no Germanic warrior could cross the Rhine without causing a reaction by Rome. When some Celtic allies of the Suebi then attacked the Aedui, Caesar had no choice but to attack Ariovistus. In the ensuing Battle of Vesontio (58 BC), the Suebi were heavily defeated: they lost thousands of men and the few survivors were obliged to flee across the Rhine in order to save their lives.

In 57 BC, another quarrel between Celtic tribes gave Caesar the opportunity to start a new campaign. This time the menace for Rome's Gallic allies was represented by the Belgae, a powerful confederation of Celtic tribes living in the northern part of Gaul (in present-day Belgium). The Belgae were extremely strong militarily but had experienced very little contact with the Mediterranean world, being heavily influenced by the Germanic tribes living on the other side of the Rhine. The Belgae confederation had been formed during 58 BC in order to balance Caesar's increasing political influence over Gaul, but this move had been perceived as a menace by the Aedui and the other local allies of Rome, who feared that such a powerful confederation could conquer most of Gaul. Caesar's military operations against the Belgae proved extremely difficult, with the Romans very nearly defeated at the Battle of the Sabis in 57 BC. This encounter, however, proved to be decisive for the destiny of the Belgae. After securing his hard-earned victory, Caesar was able to conquer most of the enemy's settlements and gradually crushed the resistance of the Belgae, who had lost most of their best warriors in the earlier battle. By the end of the year, all the territories of the Belgae were in Roman hands. Consequently, it became clear to Caesar's Celtic allies, such as the Aedui, that the Romans were gradually conquering the whole territory of Gaul by using the internal divisions of the Celts. In 56 BC, Caesar moved against the Celts of Armorica on the northern Atlantic coast of Gaul, who had formed a tribal confederation following the example of the Belgae. This also included the important tribe of the Veneti, the only Celtic community to have seafaring capabilities and a fleet of warships. The campaign fought against them proved to be a very difficult one for Caesar, who had to build a fleet on the English Channel and fight with all his resources both on land and at sea. Thanks to an intelligent use of innovative amphibious tactics, the Romans were finally able to prevail over the Armorican Celts and defeated them in Normandy. Following these events, the year 55 BC was employed by Caesar to mount two punitive expeditions on the borders of Gaul: one against the Germani and the other against the Britons. After the defeat of Ariovistus and his Suebi, other Germanic tribes living on the eastern bank of the Rhine had continued to mount frequent raids against Gaul. In order to show to his Celtic allies that he was still the 'protector' of Gaul, Caesar decided to organize a punitive campaign against the Germani and thus crossed the Rhine to punish the raiders on their own territories. Both the Germani and the Celts were highly impressed by Caesar's subsequent actions, the Romans building a massive bridge over the Rhine and crossing the river with large military forces. No other leader, Roman or Celtic, had ever achieved such a feat: the Germanic tribes were taken by surprise and were defeated quite easily.

As we have seen, the most prominent military leader of the Germani during the time of Julius Caesar was Ariovistus of the Suebi. In this regard, it is important to note that after the events of the Cimbrian War, the Germani turned their attention to the west and thus to Gaul, having realized that migration and expansion towards the south were impossible due to the presence of the Roman forces that defended the Alps. Gaul was inhabited by several different tribes and was extremely fragmented politically: as a result, it looked like a perfect land of conquest for the Germani who lived on the eastern bank of the Rhine. Ariovistus was one of the Germanic leaders who tried to settle his own communities in Gaul by conquering new territories there. Unluckily for them, the Suebi made this move while Julius Caesar and his legions were gradually conquering Gaul from the south. This period was a very dramatic one for the Celts of present-day France, since they had to fight against the Germani on one side and the Romans on the other. The Germani had stronger military forces than the Celts, but were unable to conquer Gaul due to Caesar's political moves. Caesar presented himself as the 'saviour of Gaul' and thereby obtained the support of many Celts in his struggle against the Germani. It is impossible to know just how events would have panned out if Gaul had been conquered by the Germanic tribes and not by the Romans. Nevertheless, it is clear that by around 55 BC, the expansionism of the Germani produced a mass-migration of the Suebi towards the Celtic territories of the west.

Initially, Ariovistus was an ally of Rome, receiving from the Senate the honorific title of *rex Germanorum* ('King of the Germani'). Indeed, he exerted control over all the Germanic communities that had settled on the borders of Gaul along the Rhine. Ariovistus, however, pursued the interests of his tribe and not those of Rome. Around 64 BC, shortly before the arrival of Caesar, Gaul was in turmoil, with the three most important Celtic 'nations' inhabiting its territory at war against each other. The Arverni and the Sequani had established a strong military alliance and had started to attack the Aedui, who had been Rome's main allies in Gaul for decades and thus could count on the material support of the Republic. The territory of the Aedui was located between the areas inhabited by the Arverni and the Sequani. As a result, if the Aedui had been defeated, their lands would have been partitioned between the victors. The Arverni and the Sequani wanted to control the main waterways of France in order to obtain supremacy over the most important commercial routes of Gaul. Ariovistus and his Suebi took advantage of this conflict that ravaged a large portion of present-day France by forming an alliance with the Arverni and the Sequani. In 63 BC, the Suebi crossed the Rhine in great numbers and joined forces with their new Celtic allies. Soon after, the decisive Battle of Magetobriga was fought in north-eastern Gaul. We know very little of this clash, which was the greatest battle ever fought between two Celtic armies; according to ancient sources, Ariovistus participated at the head of 15,000 Suebi warriors. The Suebi played a prominent role during the clash and showed all their military superiority, turning the tide of the battle in favour of their allies. The events that took place at Magetobriga were extremely important for the history of Gaul: after the battle, the Aedui were forced to become vassals of the Sequani, while the Suebi were permitted to settle on the western bank of the Rhine. These consequences were impossible to accept for Rome, who had supported the Aedui during the conflict but with insufficient resources. The arrival of the

Germanic warrior in winter dress. (*Photo and copyright by Ancient Thrace*)

Cheruscan warrior with club and hexagonal shield. (*Photo and copyright by Ancient Thrace*)

Germani in Gaul revolutionized the political situation of the region and the balance of power that the Romans had gradually created. From many points of view, the Battle of Magetobriga was the real *casus belli* that provoked the subsequent Roman military intervention in Gaul. Soon after being defeated, the Aedui sent ambassadors to Rome and asked for help against their enemies. Meanwhile, Ariovistus was given one-third of the land previously inhabited by the Sequani in exchange for his military intervention and was permitted to settle 120,000 Suebi in Gaul, on territory not far from the Rhine.

Once the Germanic presence in Gaul had become quite significant, Ariovistus decided to turn against his former allies and attacked the Sequani. His warriors raided and terrorized all the Celtic settlements of north-eastern Gaul, in search of lands where new immigrants from the eastern bank of the Rhine could settle. Ariovistus' demands for another third of the Sequani's lands were unacceptable and caused a reaction from most of the Celtic communities. Soon after the Battle of Magetobriga, it became clear that the Germani had only entered Gaul to assume complete dominance over the region and not to act as simple allies of the Arverni and Sequani. Initially, the Romans tried to establish a positive relationship with Ariovistus, giving him the honorific title of 'King of the Germani' and recognizing his supremacy over parts of Gaul. In reality, however, the Republic was just preparing for war against the Germani in view of future expansionist moves that would take place in Gaul. In 58 BC, Caesar arrived in Gaul and sent his ambassadors to summon Ariovistus to a conference, but the leader of the Germani refused to meet the Roman general. Caesar responded to this 'offence' by sending his ambassadors to Ariovistus' camp once more, this time with a precise series of requests: the Germani were formally forbidden to transfer more families to the western back of the Rhine, were required to bring back all the hostages that they had obtained from the Aedui after the Battle of Magetobriga and were forbidden to wage war on any Celtic tribe (especially on the Aedui). Ariovistus was offended by Caesar's requests, since he wanted to assert his right to exact tributes and take hostages from the defeated Aedui. The Suebi rapidly prepared themselves for war and established their main base at Vesontio, in a location that had been particularly important for the Aedui from a commercial point of view.

Caesar advanced with his forces towards Vesontio and, before attacking the Germani, tried to come to terms with Ariovistus. The Romans' position in Gaul was not yet very strong, and thus the ambitious general probably wanted to avoid a direct confrontation with the warlike Suebi. After a long meeting, which came to nothing, both Caesar and Ariovistus returned to their respective camps and prepared for battle. The Germanic leader perfectly understood that Caesar had come to Gaul only

Germanic skirmisher equipped with javelin and oval shield. (*Photo and copyright by Ancient Thrace*)

Germanic warrior armed with sword. (*Photo and copyright by Ancient Thrace*)

Cheruscan warrior; note the pointed umbo of the shield. (*Photo and copyright by Ancient Thrace*)

Goth warrior carrying round shield. (*Photo and copyright by Ancient Thrace*)

near Vercingetorix's capital. The Celts were able to prevail, and for the first time they defeated the Romans in a great battle, albeit suffering heavy losses and thus being unable to effectively pursue Caesar. Both sides then needed time to reorganize their forces; Vercingetorix, in particular, was waiting for the arrival of massive reinforcements from other areas of Gaul. As a result, he decided to concentrate his troops in the most important stronghold of Gaul: Alesia, a fortified city that was considered unconquerable by most contemporary observers. After reorganizing his forces, Caesar marched to besiege Alesia and built a first wall around the city in order to isolate the defenders from outside aid. However, a massive army of 100,000 Celtic warriors arrived to reinforce Vercingetorix's forces. Caesar now risked being trapped between two large Gallic armies, one surrounding his forces and the other being stationed inside Alesia. As a result, he ordered the construction of a second wall to protect his legions from the assaults of the Celtic reinforcements. The joint attacks of the Gauls, mounted from the inside as well as from the outside, almost achieved victory for the Gauls. The Roman defences were very nearly broken and only a desperate counter-attack launched by Caesar himself with his last reserves saved the legions from total defeat. After the failure of these assaults, the Gallic reinforcements were routed and abandoned Vercingetorix to his fate. The great Gallic leader finally surrendered when he ran out of supplies, after a courageous but hopeless resistance. He was held prisoner for several years, then killed during Caesar's triumph through Rome for conquering Gaul.

The armies of Caesar that conquered most of Gaul inside a few years did not comprise only Roman legionaries; they were supported by a series of auxiliary contingents that were made up of non-Roman professional soldiers. These could be mercenaries or allies who were extremely loyal to Caesar, and performed some specific tactical functions. It is important to remember that with the military reforms carried out by Gaius Marius during the Cimbrian War, the Roman legions had adopted a new structure that did not comprise light infantry but only *cohortes* of heavy infantry. As a result of this, the Romans had to rely on foreign soldiers in order to deploy sizeable contingents of light troops. The same happened for the cavalry, which had never been a fundamental component of the Roman Army. During his Gallic campaigns, Caesar deployed the following auxiliary contingents: Celtic heavy cavalry, Germanic light cavalry, mounted skirmishers recruited from the Numidians and the Mauri, Cretan archers, Balearic slingers and Iberian light infantry. The Celtic heavy cavalry came from the tribes of Gaul that were allied with Rome, most notably from the Aedui. They were equipped with helmet and chainmail, and were armed with spears and long slashing swords. Mounted on tall horses, these cavalrymen made up a 'shock' force that was employed by Caesar on

Goth warrior. (*Photo and copyright by Ancient Thrace*)

several occasions and with great success. The Germanic light cavalry, meanwhile, were equipped as light skirmishers: they did not carry armour or helmets and were armed with throwing javelins. These horsemen were of great use in conducting reconnaissance missions as well as harassing the enemy with rapid incursions. On some occasions, they were also employed to launch frontal charges, and were always considered by Caesar as a fundamental component of his forces. In 55 BC, the Roman troops operating in Gaul included a total of 400 Germani, who were all nobles from the tribes that had been defeated by Caesar and who served alongside the Romans (together with their servants) as hostages. Their presence on Rome's side was a sign of good will and trust, which had great political importance. Caesar was particularly impressed by the martial spirit of the Germani, admiring them for their courage and their simple way of life, which was ideal to forge good warriors. The 400 Germanic cavalrymen who served as part of Caesar's army were supported by a number of light infantrymen: these were the servants of the Germanic nobles and were trained to run together with the horsemen in order to cover their flanks during close combat. Caesar encountered this peculiar tactical formation invented by the Germani during the campaign fought against Ariovistus, and soon saw that it had great potential. As a result, he was the first commander to create some combined units of infantry and cavalry inside the Roman Army. These later became known as *cohortes equitate* and

Goth warriors in wedge formation. (*Photo and copyright by Ancient Thrace*)

Warrior of the Suebi; note the torque worn around the neck. (*Photo and copyright by Ancient Thrace*)

Germanic skirmisher equipped with throwing javelin. (*Photo and copyright by Ancient Thrace*)

remained an important component of the Roman military for a long time. The light infantrymen of the Germani ran alongside the cavalry, clinging to the manes of their horses, and were mostly tasked with stabbing at enemy mounts. With the outbreak of Vercingetorix's rebellion, many 'allied' Celtic horsemen abandoned Caesar, so he was obliged to recruit more Germani (from the eastern bank of the Rhine) in order to replace them. These numbered some 600, as usual accompanied by their servants as light infantrymen. The Germanic warriors of Caesar fought with enormous valour on several occasions against Vercingetorix's forces, always routing the Celtic cavalry that opposed them. The Germani who participated in the final Gallic campaign of 52 BC also followed Caesar during the ensuing years, taking part in all the conflicts that were fought by their general, most notably the civil war that ended with the defeat of Pompey at the Battle of Pharsalus. In 45 BC, Caesar returned to Rome and disbanded the auxiliary corps of his army. The surviving Germanic veterans went back to their homeland, after having travelled around the Mediterranean and plundered in many different countries. The Numidians and the Mauri serving with Caesar were equipped as mounted skirmishers and used javelins as their main weapon. As they had done as part of Hannibal's Carthaginian army, they performed as explorers and were masters in organizing ambushes. Cretan archers and Balearic slingers were all mercenaries, well known in the Mediterranean world for their incredible fighting skills. Crete and the Balearic Islands were the home of two of the most important 'light infantry schools' of Antiquity, where the deadliest archers and slingers were trained as professional soldiers from childhood. The Iberian light infantrymen were known as *caetrati*, because they carried a small round shield that was called the *caetra*. Armed with deadly short swords and javelins, Caesar appreciated them for their great tactical flexibility. Apparently, the Roman armies in Gaul also comprised a small number of Iberian cavalrymen, who had heavy personal equipment like their Celtic equivalents.

Chapter 4

The Campaigns of Augustus in Germania

In 44 BC, at the time of Julius Caesar's assassination in the Senate, Gaul had been completely conquered by the Roman Republic, which now had a very long border with the lands inhabited by the Germani that were collectively called 'Germania' by the Romans. Until 30 BC, the military situation remained extremely quiet on the Rhine frontier, since the Romans were heavily involved in the civil wars that followed the death of Caesar. These ended only with the final victory of Augustus, who emerged as the first Emperor of Rome and gradually transformed the Republic into a Principate. During the years that saw the consolidation of Augustus' personal power, several of the Celtic tribes in Gaul revolted against Rome and tried to restore their autonomy, but these local rebellions were all easily crushed by the Romans and peace reigned again in Gaul by 27 BC. Augustus, however, was greatly irritated by the fact that the Celtic revolts had received material and ideological support from the Germanic tribes on the eastern bank of the Rhine. Consequently, he decided to secure the Roman military presence along the Rhine by building new fortifications in the area and severely punishing all those Germani who had helped the Gallic rebels. Augustus was gradually developing the idea of *limes*, a fortified border, although he believed the Roman legions could easily conquer most of Germania thanks to their military superiority. The emperor also felt that the cultural superiority of Roman civilization could neutralize the Germani: they could be transformed from wild 'barbarians' to civilized subjects of the Roman Empire, as had already been done with most of the Celts living in Gaul. During the long reign of Augustus, the Romans absorbed several small client kingdoms into the Empire by forming a 'social alliance' with the local aristocracies. The nobles of the various protectorates were permitted to continue ruling over their lands but were required to send their sons to the capital of the Empire to receive a perfect Roman education. Upon returning to their homeland, these 'client princes' were charged with the task of favouring the incorporation of their territory into the Empire and would govern it as a province for Rome. Augustus also wanted to use this method of indirect conquest for Germania, but as we will see, his plans were to fail completely.

In 16 BC, the Romans were given the *casus belli* that they needed to initiate military operations in Germania. Three tribes living on the eastern bank of the Rhine crossed

Frankish warrior with club and hexagonal shield. (*Photo and copyright by Ancient Thrace*)

Suebian skirmisher. (*Photo and copyright by Ancient Thrace*)

the frontier and attacked Roman units garrisoning the border. The Roman V Legion was taken by surprise and defeated by the Germanic raiders, who were even able to capture its eagle, the most sacred insignia of a legion. This unexpected defeat persuaded Augustus to transform Gaul into an immense military camp and to begin preparations for an invasion of Germania, as he believed the recent turn of events had shown that Gaul could only be considered completely safe after the elimination of the potential menace represented by the Germani. The tribes that had been responsible for the raids and the defeat of the Roman forces were soon pushed back to the eastern bank of the Rhine, and then sent envoys to Augustus begging for peace. However, Augustus was by now ready to implement his expansionistic policy towards Germania. Taxes were collected from every corner of Gaul to finance the upcoming military expeditions, and a mint was established at Lugdunum (modern Lyon) in order to produce the coinage that was needed to pay the legionaries who would be operating in Germania. Drusus, a general with great combat experience and a stepson of Augusts, was made governor of Gaul in 13 BC. He would be the main commander of the Roman forces tasked with invading Germania. Soon after his appointment, however, Drusus had to face a series of minor rebellions in Gaul that were caused by the new taxation imposed by the Romans. While crushing the Gallic revolts, Drusus also had to repulse a Germanic raid from the eastern bank of the Rhine: he reacted to this by launching a retaliatory attack across the river, which caused significant losses to the Germani.

During 12 and 11 BC, Drusus operated in north-western Germany with great success. He invaded the land of the Usipetes and pillaged the territory of the Sicambri, two of the tribes that had attacked Gaul. He then moved to the territory of the present-day Netherlands, where the local Germanic communities of the Batavi and the Frisians were easily submitted. These soon became loyal 'clients' of Rome, providing soldiers for the Roman *auxilia* units and even sending some chosen warriors who made up Augustus' personal bodyguard. The first Emperor of Rome was the creator of the famous Praetorian Guard and the other military corps that garrisoned the capital. Augustus also organized a small Germanic bodyguard that was totally independent from the Praetorians: the *Germani corporis custodes*. This was entirely composed of Germanic warriors of the Batavian tribe, who acted as personal protectors of the emperor and his family. They were extremely loyal to Augustus and, being foreigners, had no links with the political parties involved in the Roman power struggles. In AD 9, as a result of the defeat of the Roman general Varus in Germania, the unit was temporarily disbanded. It was reformed after a few years, only to be disbanded again in AD 69 by Galba because of its strong loyalty towards Nero (who had just died). Initially, the Germanic guards provided by the Batavi were only some 100 strong, but by the time of Nero there were 500 of them organized in *decuriae* ('tens'), each led by an officer known as a decurion. After securing Roman dominance over the Batavi and the Frisians, Drusus moved along the northern coast of Germania and attacked the Chauci. Obtaining some other minor successes, he returned to Gaul due to the coming of winter. In just a few months, without experiencing significant military difficulties, the Romans had occupied the whole territory of the modern Netherlands and punished the most important Germanic tribes living near the Rhine for their incursions into Gaul.

During the following spring, Drusus launched another campaign in Germania. Rapidly subduing the Usipetes, he then marched east to the River Weser. The Romans were by this time already in the heart of Germania, where the important tribe of the Cherusci lived. The Cherusci controlled a large portion of territory located between the rivers Ems and Elbe. No Roman general had ever advanced so deeply into Germania, so Drusus was moving in a completely unknown land. With the coming of winter, not being sure of the subdued Germani's loyalty towards the Empire, Drusus returned to Gaul without having submitted the Cherusci. During the withdrawal, the Romans were attacked by small parties of Germanic warriors who harassed their columns using hit-and-run tactics. These caused significant losses to the legionaries, who were obliged to move very slowly on terrain that was largely unknown to them. At that time, the Rhine marked a frontier of civilizations between Gaul and Germania: in Gaul there were roads and *oppida* (urban settlements) built by the Celts, while in Germania the population lived in isolated settlements and no roads existed. Most of the Germanic lands were covered by impenetrable forests, characterized by a very humid climate and the presence of swamps. The heavy-armoured legionaries always had great difficulties in travelling across Germania, since their slow columns and heavy equipment needed proper roads to move rapidly. In the spring of 10 BC, after having been elected consul, Drusus again crossed again the Rhine and returned with his troops into Germania. This time he concentrated his efforts against the powerful tribe of the Chatti, who lived south of the Germanic communities that had already been subdued during the previous campaigns. The Romans were once again able to subdue the Germani and obtain some local victories, but the new successes of Drusus were not decisive. At the end of each Germanic campaign, the legionaries retreated back to Gaul without leaving behind any garrison that could control the newly submitted territories. In reality, the military campaigns of Drusus were just 'demonstrations' aimed at transforming the Germanic leaders into vassal kings rather than proper invasions to permanently conquer new provinces. The logistical difficulties experienced by the Romans prevented them from establishing a fixed military presence in Germania. All the gains obtained during each spring and

Cheruscan warrior with long club. (*Photo and copyright by Ancient Thrace*)

Germanic warrior equipped with club and shield. (*Photo and copyright by Ancient Thrace*)

summer were lost during the cold months, and thus the Germani could not truly be considered to be submitted.

In 9 BC, Drusus began his fourth Germanic campaign, again attacking the Chatti who had not been completely submitted by the Romans during the previous encounters. This new campaign was particularly difficult for Drusus and his forces, since they had to stop and fight several times during their march. The Romans once more reached the land of the Cherusci and mounted a new attack that was much more massive than the previous one and obliged the Germanic tribe to fall back to the River Elbe. The legions crossed most of the large territory inhabited by the Cherusci and devastated it, pillaging and looting with great violence. Drusus understood that the Cherusci were the strongest Germanic community living in the central part of Germania; by crushing their spirit, he hoped to gain the respect of all the other tribes. With the Romans in close pursuit and running the risk of being massacred, the Cherusci had no choice but to come to terms with Drusus. They recognized, at least formally, the suzerainty of Rome over their homeland. However, the Romans were once again obliged to leave Germania with the coming of winter, and thus their supremacy over the lands of the Cherusci was only temporary. During his four Germanic campaigns, Drusus had been able to obtain several victories over the Germani, but these successes were more the result of his enemy's internal divisions than his own military ability. The various Germanic tribes were extremely fragmented politically and spent most of their energies in bloody inter-tribal conflicts. As a result, the Romans could create alliances with single tribes and use the local rivalries to their advantage. Attacking the various Germanic communities one by one, the Romans always had a numerical superiority over their enemy and could prevail thanks to the perfect discipline of their legions. The campaigns of Drusus, however, had also shown the Romans the dangers that could be encountered in Germania. It was an unknown and savage land, where Roman armies could not fight with their usual tactics and where the terrain was an 'ally' of the local populations. Drusus had been intelligent enough to follow Caesar's example and had used the tribal divisions of his opponents to obtain several victories, according to the famous principle of *divide et impera*. Yet due to logistical difficulties, he had been obliged to abandon his conquest every year with the coming of winter, and thus the Roman presence in Germania remained a temporary one. On his way back to the Rhine at the end of his fourth Germanic campaign, Drusus fell from his horse and was badly wounded. His injury soon became seriously infected and a month later, the great Roman general died from gangrene.

Augustus, soon after hearing that Drusus was seriously ill, decided to send Tiberius to Germania as the new leader of the Roman forces operating across the Rhine. Tiberius, brother of Drusus, was militarily inexperienced but was extremely loyal to the emperor, who believed he would soon learn from experience. During 8 and 7 BC, Tiberius fought two campaigns in Germania, continuing what his brother had started. The efforts of the future emperor were mostly directed against the Sicambri, a tribe that put up a strong resistance against the Romans. Tiberius had to use all his military resources to defeat these Germani, who used guerrilla tactics to slow down the advances of the legionaries and cause them significant losses. The Romans responded with harsh repressive methods, which included mass exterminations and the deportation of many Sicambri to the western bank of the Rhine. Tiberius was sure that these Germani would have simply continued to revolt if the Romans permitted them to remain in their homeland. After the end of Tiberius' second Germanic campaign, Roman propaganda presented western Germania as a pacified region of the Empire. However, as subsequent events on the eastern bank of the Rhine would show, this was not true. Most of the Germanic tribes who had been defeated by the legions had only accepted Roman supremacy on paper, and thus continued to act as autonomous communities. In addition, the Romans had no fortifications or significant garrisons in Germania that could control the territory and prevent the

Frankish warrior. (*Photo and copyright by Ancient Thrace*)

Frankish skirmisher. (*Photo and copyright by Ancient Thrace*)

outbreak of rebellions. Some of the most important Germanic tribes, living in the eastern part of Germania, had not been reached by the Romans, and most of Central Europe was still completely free from the political influence of the Empire.

In 6 BC, Tiberius returned to Rome and was replaced as Roman military commander on the Rhine by Lucius Domitius Ahenobarbus, who resumed the Roman offensives in Germania and rapidly moved east, crossing the Elbe. Ahenobarbus, a skilled military commander, soon understood the importance of building effective infrastructure in order to secure stable control over Germanic territory. He ordered his military engineers to build causeways across all the swamps in the region between the Rhine and the Ems, thereby allowing the Roman legions to reach the Ems much more rapidly than before. The building of these *pontes longi*, which would soon be connected by a road according to Ahenobarbus' plans, was perceived as a clear act of hostility by the Cherusci who lived in the area. After establishing some permanent infrastructure, the Romans would have been able to deploy strong military garrisons in the region. As a result, in 2 BC, the Cherusci rose up in revolt against the Romans and started to attack the parties of legionaries that patrolled their homeland. It should be noted, however, that not all the members of this Germanic tribe were in favour of a new war against Rome. While most of the common warriors hated the Romans and hoped to expel them from their territory, some of the aristocracy were becoming increasingly interested in the new commercial possibilities offered by the arrival of the newcomers. The Rhine, after Julius Caesar's conquest of Gaul, was not perceived as a real barrier by most of the peoples living on its banks: the great river was to them merely a waterway that connected different civilizations and could be used to transport commercial products. The Romans had been trading with the Germani long before the ascendancy of Augustus, and thus, now that they had a stronger presence on the western borders of Germania, many wealthy aristocrats of the Germanic tribes understood that they could become rich through trade. Some products that could be found only in Germania, such as amber, were of particular interesting to the Romans. The same could be said for other goods like wine, which were not produced in Germania but were loved by the Germani. Nevertheless, the great majority of the Cherusci were still in favour of war against Rome, and hostilities commenced. Ahenobarbus, after several minor battles, did not obtain a significant victory over the Cherusci, and thus was rapidly replaced by the emperor. In 2 BC, Augustus sent a new military commander to Germania: the seasoned Marcus Vinicius.

Vinicius operated in Germania until AD 4, at the head of a considerable military force that comprised five legions. He spent most of his years as commander of the Roman troops in Germania quelling local rebellions and marching across the Rhine to

Goth warrior with spear and round shield. (*Photo and copyright by Ancient Thrace*)

Germanic warrior of the Rhine frontier. (*Photo and copyright by Ancient Thrace*)

consolidate the imperial presence on the eastern bank of the great river. He obtained several victories, but none of them were decisive as the Germani always avoided facing the Romans in a large pitched clash. That same year, Augustus sent Tiberius back to the Rhine with orders to finally pacify the region. Tiberius performed extremely well during his second spell in Germania, being able to subdue several minor tribes as well as to defeat the Cherusci who were still fighting against the Romans. According to Tiberius' propaganda, the Cherusci had been completely pacified and thus they were given the new honorific title of 'friends of the Roman People'. Yet in reality, Tiberius had only established a formal alliance with part of the tribe's nobility and not with the great majority of its warriors, who still hated the Romans and their culture. In AD 5, the Romans organized a major offensive in Germania, which began with a massive attack on the Chauci and continued with a rapid advance directed towards the heart of the Germanic territories. The Roman troops taking part in the offensive mostly advanced on land, but a portion of them was transported on a newly built river fleet. The various units met on the banks of the River Elbe, where Tiberius assembled them into a single army and made a strong demonstration of force in front of the Germani. The Roman forces then returned to their starting positions without leaving any garrison in Germania. Once again, a Roman army had penetrated into Germanic territory with a rapid offensive but had been unable to defeat the Germani in a pitched battle. During the retreat, as had happened before, the Romans were attacked by Germanic warriors employing hit-and-run tactics.

Chapter 5

Arminius and the Battle of Teutoburg

The only positive result of the Roman 'demonstration' of AD 5 was that the Cherusci, after years of internal divisions and minor conflicts with the Romans, finally decided to become 'real' allies of Rome. This change of political attitude was the result of an internal political struggle that saw the clash between those nobles of the Cherusci who wanted to establish a formal alliance with Rome and those who were against such a move. The rapid campaign of Tiberius convinced the majority of the Cherusci that, at least for the moment, the Romans were too strong to be faced in militarily. In addition, the Germani had understood that by trading with the Romans, they could improve their living conditions and introduce new products to their economy. The pro-Roman party of the Cherusci tribe was guided by a powerful clan, whose members included a young aristocrat named Arminius. He was a 'prince', since his father was one of the most important leaders of the Cherusci and one of the main supporters of the new pro-Roman policy. Tiberius supported the pro-Roman Cherusci and Arminius' clan in every possible way, in order to transform the Cherusci into Rome's most important Germanic allies. To sustain his local allies and keep an eye on the Cherusci who still resented Roman rule, he built a strong winter base on the River Lippe. For the first time, the Romans now had a sizeable garrison in Germania. By AD 6, the Romans were exerting some form of direct or indirect influence over the entire western part of Germania; all the tribes living west of the River Elbe recognized (at least formally) the supremacy of Rome. In south-eastern Germany, west of the Elbe, there was just one Germanic tribe that had not yet submitted to the Romans: the Marcomanni, guided by their 'king' Maroboduus, who were without doubt the strongest of all the Germani militarily. The Romans, having complete control over all the other Germanic communities, planned a massive pincer attack on the Marcomanni that would involve a total of twelve legions. Before this could materialize, however, the Romans had to face a bloody uprising in the western Balkans, and the forces assembled for the campaign against the Marcomanni had to be moved to the province of Illyricum. As a result, the Empire concluded a temporary peace treaty with the Marcomanni and recognized Maroboduus as their legitimate leader. As Tiberius, who had guided with great intelligence the Roman troops in Germania, assumed command of those fighting in

Frankish warrior with hexagonal shield. (*Photo and copyright by Ancient Thrace*)

Goth warriors. (*Photo and copyright by Ancient Thrace*)

the western Balkans, a new commander had to be chosen by Augustus to replace him. This was Publius Quintilius Varus.

Before describing the events that would lead to the worst military defeat ever suffered by the Romans in Germania, it is important to understand who Arminius and Varus were. The Germanic prince, born in 18 or 17 BC, was the son of a powerful noble of the Cherusci tribe. Following Drusus' campaign against the Cherusci of 9 BC, he was sent to Rome as a 'hostage'. As has been seen in the previous chapter, Augustus wanted to apply in Germania his policy of cultural conquest that had already been employed by the Romans with other client princes. By educating these in Rome and by showing them the superiority of the Roman civilization, the emperor hoped to obtain a peaceful submission of their home territories after these princes returned to their 'nations' to rule as vassals of Rome. Arminius was raised in Rome and educated as a perfect Roman youth: he entered the ranks of the army at a very young age and learned practically everything about Roman culture. From the beginning of his military career, Arminius demonstrated a great charisma and incredible personal capabilities. As reward for his military services, he was granted Roman citizenship and was made part of the *equites* social class (inferior only to that of the senatorial aristocracy). During the Illyrian Revolt that broke out in AD 6, he served under Tiberius, commanding a unit of mounted *auxilia* that was made up of Germanic soldiers. Augustus was impressed by the loyalty and combat skills of Arminius, who fought with distinction on several occasions during the Illyrian Revolt. As a result, the emperor ordered the Germanic prince to return to his homeland and to act as the personal aide of the new governor, Publius Quintilius Varus.

Varus came from a senatorial family of Rome and had been consul in 13 BC together with Tiberius, of whom he was a personal friend. He had married Vipsania, one of the daughters of Agrippa, who was Augustus' most trusted general and greatest friend. As a result of these connections, Varus had a brilliant career in the Roman administration despite being inept in many aspects. During the years from 7–4 BC, he acted as the Roman governor of Syria and soon showed all his personal limits: he had no respect for the traditions of the peoples living in the territory of his province, and his response to all problems was harsh repression. In addition, he increased taxes significantly and was used to augmenting his personal fortune by using illegal practices. In 4 BC, soon after the death of the local Roman client king Herod the Great, a popular revolt broke out in Judaea and Varus was forced to intervene with the four legions that were under his command in Syria. After occupying Jerusalem, he crushed the rebels with a violence that had never been seen before in Judaea: without any formal process, Varus crucified 2,000 Jewish insurgents and committed a series of pointless atrocities. These events led to the development of a strong anti-Roman sentiment in Judaea and caused Varus' removal from the governorship of Syria. In AD 6, after a period of disgrace, Varus was appointed governor of Germania and sent to the northern borders of the Empire. His main task was to organize the newly conquered lands into a proper Roman province, in order to formalize their annexation to the Empire. Considering his personal background and previous career, Varus was not the right man to achieve such a difficult objective. He had little military experience, no knowledge of Germania and was a terrible administrator. The governorship of Germania was a 'second chance' for him and his career, which he was able to obtain only thanks to his personal connections. Augustus knew this very well, and thus decided to send Arminius to Germania in order to give Varus an expert and reliable 'adjutant'.

When Varus arrived in Germania, the Roman forces deployed on the Rhine had been greatly reduced in number. Most the units stationed on the borders of Gaul had been sent to the western Balkans in order to fight against the local insurgents. As a result, only three legions were available for campaigning in Germania (the XVII, XVIII and XIX). These legions did not have a very long military tradition, since they had been formed only during the last phase of the Roman civil wars. In addition, with the exception of the XIX Legion, they had never fought for long periods in Germania. After returning to his homeland, Arminius soon became a trusted advisor to Varus, who knew practically nothing about Germania and had to rely on Arminius to take all the most important operational decisions. After a few months of his governorship in Germania, Varus clearly showed he had learned very little from his previous mistakes: he started to impose a very heavy taxation on the Germanic tribes and began using very harsh repressive methods to ensure the loyalty of his new subjects. The insolence and cruelty of Varus were intolerable for the Germani, who still considered themselves as free individuals and had accepted the Roman presence on their territories only for practical reasons. The taxes imposed by the new governor were impossible to sustain, while the violence of the occupiers caused the death of many civilians. Within a few months, the Germani had lost their beloved freedom and found themselves with an army of occupation on their homeland. Arminius, disgusted by the conduct of Varus and his love for gold, gradually came to realize that the Germani would never flourish as a people under such an inept governor and decided that it was better for them to be independent from Rome than being treated like animals. Despite having spent most of his life in Rome, the Germanic prince still loved his homeland and its inhabitants: a Roman education had not cancelled his true Germanic spirit, as had been hoped by Augustus. The Romans had taught all their military practices to a man who was now going to become one of their worst enemies. Learning from recent history, Arminius understood that the Germani had never been able to prevail over the Romans because they had always been fragmented, both politically and militarily. Now, with Varus in Germania, the only way to defeat and expel the Romans was to create a large inter-tribal confederation of Germani that would be able to deploy a massive Germanic army.

Arminius had secret meetings with the leaders of the major Germanic tribes, and thanks to his personal charisma was able to convince them of the necessity of creating a major alliance. As most of the Germanic tribes were divided by strong rivalries, it was not easy for Arminius to erase the memories of the recent past in order to propose a new vision to all the Germani. In the end, six major tribes of western Germania decided to support Arminius' plans: the Cherusci, Marsi, Chatti, Bructeri, Chauci and Sicambri. These were supplemented by the surviving elements of the Suebi who

Alemannic warrior with long club. (*Photo and copyright by Ancient Thrace*)

Suebian warrior. (*Photo and copyright by Ancient Thrace*)

still lived in Germania and had not been crushed by Caesar. After cementing the Germanic inter-tribal alliance, Arminius waited for the right moment to strike while continuing to act as Varus' main adjutant. In AD 9, during the early days of September, Varus moved with his three legions from a newly built summer camp on the River Weser to his winter headquarters that were located not far from the Rhine. During the march, Varus was informed of the outbreak of a local revolt not far from his current position. Both the uprising and the reports of its effects were fabricated by Arminius, who wanted to make the legions leave their usual path and enter a densely forested area where he could ambush them with his Germanic warriors. Varus ordered Arminius to guide him to the area of the rebellion, since he had no knowledge of the terrain that the legions were crossing. Arminius directed the Romans along a route that was completely unfamiliar to them. Another Cheruscan nobleman, a personal enemy of Arminius named Segestes, tried to warn Varus about the possibility that the Roman legions could be ambushed, and even accused Arminius of being a traitor. Segestes' warnings, however, were dismissed by Varus, who considered them as merely the result of the personal feud existing between the two Cheruscan noblemen. After these events, Arminius left the Roman column under the pretext of assembling some Germanic forces that would support the Romans in crushing the supposed rebellion.

In reality, the Cheruscan leader went to the defensive positions that his Germanic warriors had prepared in the surrounding woods and assumed command of his forces. The deadly ambush organized by Arminius took place at Kalkriese Hill, in Lower Saxony, not far from present-day Detmond. Varus' troops not only comprised the three legions mentioned above, but also six infantry *cohortes* and three cavalry *alae* of auxiliaries. These, like most of the legionaries, did not have any great combat experience. The Roman soldiers did not march in combat formation, since they were convinced they were moving in safe territory where they would not be attacked. Furthermore, the various military units were interspersed with several hundred civilian camp followers. These included the families of the legionaries and the auxiliaries, as well as merchants and other workers who lived with the soldiers in their camps. In total, the Roman force comprised around 19,000 soldiers, together with 4,000–5,000 non-combatants. Following Arminius' indications, the Roman column started to follow a path that crossed a densely forested area. As they continued to advance, the path became increasingly narrow and muddy. Expecting no attacks from the local Germanic tribes, Varus did not send any cavalry explorers ahead of his main column, and even continued his march after a violent storm began. The Roman column was gradually and dangerously becoming too long and too slow due to the broken terrain that it was crossing. By now, the column was some 20km long, so the units marching at its head could not communicate rapidly with those bringing up the rear. When

Goth warrior. (*Photo and copyright by Ancient Thrace*)

Border skirmish between Germanic tribal warriors. (*Photo and copyright by Ancient Thrace*)

the legions were stretched and dispersed among the woods, the Germanic warriors of Varus emerged from the dense vegetation of the forest and started to attack the Romans. The column was taken by complete surprise, and had no time to develop any defensive formation. In any case, the limited space along the narrow path that they were following made the adoption of any combat formation practically impossible. Arminius, who had an extensive knowledge of Roman military tactics, had chosen the perfect location to organize his ambush. He ordered his warriors not to attack the Romans directly, at least not during the early phase of the battle. Instead, they skirmished with the legionaries from a distance by using their light javelins. In this early phase of the clash, hundreds of Romans were killed without even seeing their enemies.

The Germani attacked individual sections of the long Roman column, always having a decisive local superiority over their enemies. Any small group of legionaries who became isolated from the main column was rapidly surrounded by the Germanic warriors and massacred. By the end of the first day of battle, the Romans had already lost thousands of soldiers without causing any significant losses to their attackers. Under heavy rain, Varus ordered the construction of a temporary camp in the forest and spent the night in this fortified position. On the following morning, the Romans tried to leave the woods and reach an open area that was located not far from their temporary camp. However, the legionaries were attacked again by Arminius' men and were unable to fight their way out of the forest. Torrential rain did not help the Romans, who were by now starting to panic and had no idea how to deal with the situation they found themselves in. At the end of the second day of battle, the Romans set off on a night-time march towards the foot of Kalkriese Hill in the hope of installing themselves on higher ground and putting up stronger resistance against the Germani. Arminius, however, had foreseen this move, and had prepared a strong defensive position at Kalkriese Hill. The Romans had to abandon the main path and follow a sandy strip between the hill and a nearby swamp that was known as the Great Bog because of its extensive dimensions. Between Kalkriese Hill and the Great Bog there was a small gap of only 100 metres, with some dense vegetation on the left at the foot of the hill. Upon reaching this location, the Romans saw that the new path was blocked by a trench, and it was impossible for them to reach the top of the hill. At the same time, they learned that the Germani had built a solid earthen wall in the dense vegetation that covered the foot of Kalkriese Hill on their left. This permitted the Germani to attack the Romans with their throwing weapons from behind cover. Arminius had prepared the most perfect ambush: Varus and his men had no possibility of escape. At the rear of the Roman column, some 10,000 Germanic warriors were in position to prevent any retreat, while at the head of the column, the narrow path disappeared into the forest and the vegetation was too dense to permit any further advance. Meanwhile, on the right, the Romans were faced by the Great Bog, and on the left there was the earthen wall built by Arminius and defended by over 14,000 Germanic warriors.

The Germani began attacking the Romans with increasing violence, killing hundreds more of them without coming out from their fortified positions. The legionaries made a desperate attempt to storm the earthen wall, but were repulsed with severe losses. At this point, the few cavalry of the Roman column tried to flee from the trap by abandoning the foot troops, but the mounted *auxilia* were soon intercepted and massacred by the larger number of Germanic cavalry that Arminius had kept in reserve. As it became apparent that the Roman formations were collapsing, the Germani came out from their positions and launched a direct attack against the surviving legionaries. The ensuing hand-to-hand fighting was particularly violent, since the Roman soldiers had no chance of survival and could only save their honour by putting up a heroic last stand. Varus, having understood that the disaster had been produced by his ineptitude, committed suicide; his soldiers, instead, grouped themselves in various improvised defensive formations and tried to resist as long as they could. Attacked by thousands of Germani, they were slaughtered one by one, together with all the civilians who were part of the column. Most of the Roman

Alemannic warrior with club and rectangular shield. (*Photo and copyright by Ancient Thrace*)

Germanic warrior; note the hair having the traditional shape of the 'Suebian knot'. (*Photo and copyright by Ancient Thrace*)

officers committed suicide, preferring this to capture and torture. In total, more than 20,000 Romans were killed in what became known as the Battle of the Teutoburg Forest. It was one of the worst defeats ever suffered by the Roman Army, which lost three of its formidable legions in an obscure and unknown forest of Central Europe. The few surviving Romans were all captured and enslaved by the Germani, except for the officers, who were sacrificed during religious ceremonies that celebrated the great Germanic victory. Only a very few Romans were ransomed and could return to the western bank of the Rhine, where they reported to the local authorities the terrible events of the Teutoburg Forest.

Arminius had obtained a complete victory over the Romans and had practically destroyed all their military forces that were deployed in Germania. His warriors took thousands of weapons and pieces of armour from the dead legionaries and auxiliaries, in addition to the goods and money transported by the many civilians who were part of the column. When news of the Battle of the Teutoburg Forest reached the Rhine, the Roman authorities had no choice but to evacuate all the forts and garrisons that had been recently built on the eastern bank of the river. The territory of Gaul was now exposed to raids by the Germani. Only one Roman fort, built at Aliso, resisted for several weeks, repulsing all the attacks launched by the Germani. Although its garrison was eventually forced to retreat back to the Rhine like all the other Roman units, it had gained enough time to enable the legions that were stationed in Gaul to organize a defensive line along the river. At that moment, the Romans had just two legions on the frontier between Gaul and Germania, so an invasion of the Gallic territories by Arminius was greatly feared. The victorious Germanic leader, however, was fully satisfied because he had achieved his primary objective: freeing the whole territory of Germania from Roman military presence. Upon hearing of the terrible defeat suffered in Germania, Augustus was so shocked that he was reported as spending several days and nights butting his head against the walls of his palace. According to the Roman historian Suetonius, the emperor continued shouting the same phrase with a desperate tone: '*Quintili Vare, legiones redde!*' ('Quintilius Varus, give me back my legions!'). Augustus spent the last five years of his life thinking of the massacre caused by Varus, which became commonly known in Rome as *Clades Variana* ('the Varian disaster'). The three legions that had been destroyed by Arminius were never re-formed; the Romans were extremely superstitious and did not want to give a new military unit the official denomination of a corps that had been wiped out in such terrible circumstances.

After the Battle of the Teutoburg Forest, Arminius became the supreme leader of western Germania and also increased his personal influence over those Germanic tribes that had not been part of his confederation. The Cheruscan leader considered

Cheruscan warrior. (*Photo and copyright by Ancient Thrace*)

Germanic warrior of the Rhine frontier. (*Photo and copyright by Ancient Thrace*)

his victory over the Romans only as the starting point of a larger process that would have ended with the political unification of Germania. Arminius fully understood that the Romans would soon want to attack the Germani to have their revenge, assembling a large invading force and avoiding the mistakes committed by Varus. Attempting to establish a military alliance with the powerful Marcomanni, whose leader Maroboduus was the only other 'supreme' overlord of Germania, Arminius sent them the severed head of Varus together with the offer of an anti-Roman alliance. Maroboduus, who had recently been recognized as 'king' of his tribe by the Romans, refused Arminius' offer and sent Varus' head to Rome to show his respect for the Empire. Meanwhile, the Romans sent Tiberius with three legions to Gaul and prepared for a massive counter-offensive: the honour of the Roman Army had been offended and the imperial eagles of Varus' legions were in enemy hands. As we will see in the next chapter, the Marcomanni remained neutral during the ensuing conflict between Arminius and Rome, so the Cheruscan leader had to fight alone against a superior imperial force.

From a historical point of view, the Battle of the Teutoburg Forest had an enormous importance, marking the end of the short-lived Roman presence in Germania. Following Arminius' victory, the Rhine began to mark the border between two worlds and two civilizations: the Roman and the Germanic. This cultural division of Europe is still visible today, in the languages spoken by the European peoples and in their way of thinking. No one knows how the history of the Western world could have been different if present-day Germany had been 'romanized'. What can be taken for granted is that the Germanic invasions of the Roman Empire would have never taken place, and that the eventual fall of Rome would have been completely different from the one we know (which was mostly the result of the great Germanic migrations).

Chapter 6

The *limes* of the Rhine and the Marcomannic Wars

Following the Battle of the Teutoburg Forest, Germania was in turmoil. The western part of the region was dominated by Arminius, who was waiting the return of a Roman army seeking revenge, while the eastern portion was controlled by the Marcomanni, who had transferred their communities to the territories of the present-day Czech Republic. As has been seen in the previous chapter, soon after achieving his great victory over the Romans, Arminius had tried to form an alliance with the Marcomannic leader Maroboduus, but had been snubbed. This political act was unexpected by Arminius and led to a progressive increase in tension between the Cherusci and the Marcomanni. Germania could not be ruled by two overlords, but the inter-tribal wars were postponed for the moment in view of the legions' return. Augustus was furious at the *Clades Variana*, and soon after the events of the Teutoburg he had sent Tiberius, together with significant military forces, to Germania. Apparently, the emperor wanted to attempt a reconquest of the areas that had been lost, but his future successor had other plans for the Germanic campaign that he was going to conduct. Upon reaching the Rhine in AD 10, Tiberius decided to simply stabilize the eastern frontier of Gaul and did not attempt to defeat Arminius' forces in their own territory. The Rhine fortifications were repaired and supplemented by new defensive structures, while the available garrison forces were distributed more effectively and the whole frontier region was militarized. After securing his supply lines, Tiberius did move into Germania, but only to conduct some punitive long-range raids: the Romans burned houses, devastated fields and routed all the local Germanic forces that tried to stop them. Arminius, realizing that the Romans had decided not to attempt a new invasion, remained quiet and did not attack the raiders. Tiberius moved very slowly during his new campaign in Germania, taking all the necessary precautions: he was terrified of the possibility of being ambushed like Varus, and thus did not deploy a very adventurous strategy. His advances were extremely cautious, all orders were given in writing and he had to be consulted for any decision (even the smallest ones). Tiberius was obsessed by the fear that a traitor could betray him and cause the defeat of his forces.

In AD 14, Augustus died and Tiberius returned to Rome in order to become emperor. During the previous years, his military actions in Germania had achieved

Goth warrior with spear and round shield. (*Photo and copyright by Ancient Thrace*)

Germanic warrior equipped with javelin and rectangular shield. (*Photo and copyright by Ancient Thrace*)

very little, except for punishing some local communities that had supported Arminius. Command of the Roman forces on the Rhine passed to Nero Claudius Drusus, adoptive son of Tiberius who was later known as Germanicus because of the great victories he achieved in Germania. Germanicus was the son of Drusus, who had been one of the first Roman generals campaigning in Germania (as has been seen in one of the previous chapters). Drusus was a younger brother of Tiberius, who was thus the uncle of Germanicus. The second Emperor of Rome had a real predilection for his adoptive son Germanicus, to the point of choosing him as his successor instead of his own son, Drusus Iulius Caesar. Germanicus was much more aggressive than Tiberius from the beginning of his period of command in Germania, and soon earned an excellent military reputation. He lived alongside his soldiers and faced all the same difficulties encountered by his men; for these reasons and for his simple way of life, he was particularly loved by the legionaries. With an impressive force of twelve legions under his command, Germanicus attacked the confederation of Arminius during the years AD 14–16 and obtained a series of brilliant victories. The new Roman commander did not intend to invade Germania, since this was by now considered as impossible by all Romans. He wanted instead to fight a great pitched battle against the Germani in order to crush them and eradicate the terrible memories of the Teutoburg Forest from the hearts of the Romans. Germanicus had two further objectives: finding the three imperial eagles that had been captured from Varus' legions, and killing Arminius. The Romans understood that with the death of the Cheruscan leader, the temporary unity of many of the Germani would have soon ended. The divided Germanic tribes would have remained impossible to conquer, but would have been in no position to menace the frontiers of the Empire (at least for the moment).

Germanicus mounted a rapid offensive against the lands of the Chatti and the Cherusci. He went to the site of the Battle of the Teutoburg Forest and buried the bones of the Roman soldiers that still lay on the ground several years after the disaster. This was an extremely important act symbolically, especially for the morale of the Roman Army. During this early phase of his three-year Germanic campaign, Germanicus was also able to find one of the three imperial eagles that he was searching for. The Germani did not try to stop the legions, simply conducting some minor skirmishes to harass their enemy. Eventually, however, Arminius was forced to change his strategy: the Roman legions were destroying and pillaging everything they encountered on their march, which was damaging his personal reputation as overlord of the Germanic confederation. Many of the tribes who had followed him with enthusiasm were now ready to rebel against his rule, so he had no choice but to fight against Germanicus on the open field. This took place at Idistaviso, on the right bank of the River Weser, between present-day Minden and Hamelin. Arminius deployed his forces intelligently, with the Weser between him and the legions: he was on the right bank, Germanicus on the left. Crossing the river under a rain of missile weapons thrown by the Germani would have been extremely difficult for the legions. Germanicus, however, could count on large contingents of auxiliaries from Gaul and some communities of Germanic allies (the Batavi and the Chauci) who had joined the Roman Army. Covered by the cavalry advancing in two columns, the bulk of the Roman forces were able to cross the Weser without major difficulty. One of the two Roman cavalry columns, mostly made up of Batavi, advanced deeply against the enemy positions and lost contact with the rest of Germanicus' troops. Surrounded by the Cherusci, they risked being completely destroyed. However, the exposed column linked up with the rest of the Roman cavalry and was able to retreat to safety. The main Germanic army, commanded by Arminius, left its initial positions after being unable to stop the Roman crossing of the Weser. During the following night, the Romans built a large fortified camp in the centre of the battlefield and the Germani attacked it, hoping to be helped by the darkness, but all their assaults were repulsed. On the following morning, the decisive clash between the two armies took place. First the Germani attacked, but they were repulsed with high casualties, whereupon the two Roman wings, made up of cavalry and auxiliaries, encircled the enemy and attacked them on the flanks. Arminius, seriously wounded, had no choice but to flee from the battlefield with the few survivors of his army in order to escape capture. The Battle of Idistaviso had been Germanicus' masterpiece, showing to the world that the Roman Army was still invincible on the open field and Arminius was no match for it.

Following their victory, the Romans occupied a strong defensive position that had been built by the local Germanic tribes not far from the battlefield. This, known as the Angrivarian Wall, marked the border between the territories of the Angrivarii and those of the Cherusci. Expecting a Germanic counter-attack, Germanicus dug in and waited for the arrival of the enemy. The Germani attacked the earthen wall shortly after the Romans occupied it, but all their assaults were beaten back with severe losses. After this second defeat, Arminius could no longer contain the actions of the Romans in Germania and had to deal with the rapid crumbling of the inter-tribal confederation that he had forged. The lands of the Chatti and the Marsi were devastated by Germanicus, who managed to find another imperial eagle lost at the Teutoburg. After having achieved all their objectives except for the capture of Arminius, the Romans went back to the Rhine and left Germania without attempting to occupy any territory. Their revenge had been cruel and had destroyed any possibility of Germanic political unity. In AD 17, hoping to take advantage of Arminius' weakness, the Marcomanni of Maroboduus attacked the Cherusci. This

Germanic internecine war, probably inspired by the Romans, ended in stalemate with the Marcomanni unable to achieve any significant victory. A few years later, both the main protagonists of the Battle of Idistaviso died: Germanicus was poisoned by his opponents in AD 19, while he was in Antioch, while Arminius was assassinated two years later by a rival nobleman of his own Cheruscan tribe. With the death of Arminius, any hope of Germanic political unity vanished. Nevertheless, the great warrior leader had prevented any possibility of the Romans ever conquering Germania. In AD 18, meanwhile, Maroboduus was replaced as 'king' of the Marcomanni by a younger noble who was supported by the Romans. He would die in AD 37, as an exile, in Italy.

During the following decades, up to the outbreak of the Marcomannic Wars in AD 166, the military situation on the frontier between the Roman Empire and the Germani remained relatively quiet. Some Germanic tribes occasionally launched incursions across the Rhine, to which the Romans responded with punitive raids and brief campaigns. In general, however, very little changed from a political point of view, and thus the Romans could consolidate their *limes* on the Rhine. Only one event, taking place during AD 69 and 70, saw the Romans fighting on a large scale against the Germani: the so-called Revolt of the Batavi. The Batavi had been conquered by

Germanic scout observing the enemy. (*Photo and copyright by Ancient Thrace*)

Germanic skirmisher with javelins and small shield. (*Photo and copyright by Ancient Thrace*)

the Romans several decades before and had been Rome's most loyal allies in Central Europe. They had participated in the campaign of Germanicus against Arminius, and even provided a chosen bodyguard for the emperors in Rome. In AD 69, Nero, who was particularly loved by the Batavi because he greatly appreciated their loyalty, died unexpectedly. The Roman Empire then entered into a brief but bloody phase that was characterized by civil wars. In Roman history, AD 69 is known as the 'Year of the Four Emperors', since it saw the rapid rise and fall of three new rulers who tried to take the place of Nero. This internal struggle ended with the ascendancy of Vespasian as emperor and the installation of a new dynasty, the Flavian, which replaced the original imperial family created by Augustus. The 'Year of the Four Emperors' saw the disbandment of the *Germani corporis custodes* in Rome and a rapid change in the relationship between the Romans and the Batavi. The *auxilia* units of the Batavi had played a crucial role in the Roman conquest of Britain, which commenced under Claudius. They were considered to be excellent fighters and had always been loyal to Rome.

When Nero died and the *Germani corporis custodes* were disbanded, malcontent started to spread among the Batavi, who considered this an insult to their 'national' pride. At that time, the Batavi provided eight *cohortes* of infantry and one *ala* of cavalry to the Roman Army, which were attached to the XIV Legion. When Vitellius (one of the pretenders to Nero's throne) tried to raise more troops from the Batavi for his campaigns, they rose up in revolt and attacked the legion to which their units were attached. Similarly to what happened in Germania with Arminius, the Batavian Revolt that took place in present-day Netherlands was guided by a hereditary prince who had served for a long time and with distinction in the Roman Army. He was Gaius Julius Civilis, who soon gained the upper hand in the campaign since most of the best Roman troops were fighting in the ongoing civil war. The Batavian leader was an experienced campaigner, having served as overall commander of the Batavian auxiliaries during the invasion of Britain. In the September of AD 69, the Batavi attacked the fortified camps of the two Roman legions that had been sent against them and obtained a brilliant victory, the legions forced to surrender after a long siege. The Romans were permitted to leave their camp according to the terms of a truce that was signed with Gaius Julius Civilis, but soon after having abandoned their positions, they were ambushed by the Batavi. Both legions were destroyed and most of their commanders were enslaved. After this success, the Batavi were joined by several Gallic and Germanic tribes: the Batavian Revolt was expanding, but by now the 'Year of the Four Emperors' was over and Vespasian had stabilized his control over the Empire. The new emperor assembled a massive army of eight legions to crush the rebellion. The homeland of the Batavi was invaded by the Romans, who

Goth warrior with spear and round shield. (*Photo and copyright by Ancient Thrace*)

Goth warrior with sword and round shield. (*Photo and copyright by Ancient Thrace*)

also had to fight against the Germani at sea as they had a strong fleet operating in the English Channel. Eventually, however, the Batavi were crushed and had to accept peace on humiliating terms: they lost any form of independence and their home territory started to be garrisoned on a permanent basis by Roman forces. The events of the Batavian Revolt, albeit being the result of the ongoing Roman civil war, had shown the great military potential of the Germani: a single Germanic tribe had been able to defeat two legions and regain its former autonomy.

The Marcomannic Wars, also known as the *Bellum Germanicum et Sarmaticum*, were a series of conflicts that began in AD 166 and lasted for fourteen years. They saw the clash between the Roman Army of Marcus Aurelius and the Germanic tribes of the Marcomanni and Quadi (supported by the Sarmatians, a nomadic people from the steppes of central Asia). The struggle took place on the Danubian *limes* of the Roman Empire, along which the Marcomanni had lived since the days of Maroboduus. Around AD 160, in the vast plains of Eastern Europe, an important historical event known as the Great Migrations began. This happened, at least initially, far from the eyes of the Romans, but would have had terrible consequences in the long run for the fate of the Empire. Coming under pressure from the warlike steppe peoples who were migrating across central Asia, the Germanic tribes living in Eastern Europe – such as the Goths – started to move west in search of new lands to inhabit. The steppe peoples were nomadic communities with strong military traditions: thanks to their superior cavalry forces and the deadly use of the composite bow, they were easily able to defeat the eastern Germani, obliging them to abandon their home territory. In order to avoid destruction and retain their freedom, the eastern Germani invaded the lands of the western Germani. Consequently, the western Germani were forced to cross the borders of the Roman Empire in the hope of finding new lands where they could settle. Within a few years, the Romans started to feel an increasing pressure along their frontiers that was just the beginning of a much larger historical process which would eventually cause the fall of the Empire. Until AD 160, relations between the Marcomanni and the Romans had been quite positive, since no significant conflicts had ever broke out along the western portion of the Danubian *limes*. The pressure of the Goths and the other eastern tribes, however, changed this situation. The Marcomanni tried to cross the borders of the Empire with the objective of establishing themselves in Pannonia (present-day Hungary) and the other Roman provinces that were located south of the Danube. In AD 162, the Germanic tribes of the Chatti and the Chauci moved against the western sector of the Danubian *limes*, being repulsed only after three years of incursions and combats. Then in AD 166, a group of Langobards invaded Pannonia for a short period before being crushed. These early incursions were the first signals of the beginning of a new historical process, which the Romans had not yet understood. The Marcomanni, with their leader Ballomar, initially tried to mediate between the Romans and the other Germanic tribes. However, the eastern part of the Danubian border then also came under attack. Dacia, one of the largest and most recently conquered of the Roman provinces, was invested by the Vandals and the Sarmatians, who were able to secure a decisive victory over the local military garrisons.

All these events took place in a crucial year, AD 166, which saw the emergence of another great problem for the Roman Empire. In that year, the legionaries returning from a campaign against the Parthians in Mesopotamia brought with them – inside the borders of the Empire – a new disease that became known as the 'Antonine Plague', from the name of the dynasty that was then ruling Rome (of which Marcus Aurelius was part). In just a few months, the plague killed some eight million Roman citizens and subjects, greatly weakening the Empire at a time that was already very complex for the stability of the Roman state. Marcus Aurelius reacted against the incursions of the Germanic tribes only in AD 168, when the plague ended: the economy of the Empire was in a critical situation and the Roman Army was short of men. The

Germanic warrior patrolling the territory of his tribe. (*Photo and copyright by Ancient Thrace*)

Suebian warrior. (*Photo and copyright by Ancient Thrace*)

emperor established his headquarters at Aquileia, in north-eastern Italy, and moved against the invaders of Pannonia. These had initially been repulsed, but had later been joined by the Marcomanni and returned to the Roman province during the difficult months of the spreading of the Antonine Plague. When Marcus Aurelius reached Pannonia with his forces, the Marcomanni preferred to cross back over the Danube and avoid a direct confrontation with the Romans. In AD 169, the emperor turned his attention to Dacia and fought against the Sarmatians, but obtained little success. At the same time, the Costoboci entered the Balkans from the north and raided as far as Greece. The Marcomanni, seeing an opportunity, recrossed the Danube and again invaded Pannonia with a large number of warriors. They had recently formed a strong military alliance with the Quadi, another powerful Germanic tribe.

In AD 170, at the Battle of Carnutum, the Roman forces in Pannonia were heavily defeated by the Germani, suffering over 20,000 casualties. Although there are very few details about this clash, what is known is that it was a major setback for Marcus Aurelius. After obtaining such a great and unexpected victory, the Germani ravaged Noricum (modern Austria) and moved south towards Italy. The city of Aquileia was besieged and for the first time in centuries, since the days of the Cimbrian War, the Italian peninsula was menaced by a foreign invader. By the end of AD 171, Marcus Aurelius had mounted an effective counter-offensive against the Germani. Assembling all the military resources that were available to him, he relieved Aquileia. A few months later, the invaders were repulsed on the northern bank of the Danube. At this point the Quadi signed a temporary peace treaty with Rome, while the Marcomanni continued to fight. In AD 172, Marcus Aurelius crossed the Danube and attacked Ballomar's homeland. The Roman offensive was successful, but although the Marcomanni were defeated, they still had significant military resources to deploy. The following year, the Quadi attacked the Romans again after breaking the peace treaty they had signed with the Empire. Meanwhile, the Germanic tribes of the Chatti and the Chauci launched heavy raids against the Roman *limes* on the Rhine. Marcus Aurelius concentrated all his efforts against the Quadi as he considered them, correctly, as the most serious menace to the stability of the Empire. In AD 174, the Quadi were decisively defeated, being forced to accept the presence of Roman military garrisons on their territory, surrender all prisoners and hostages who were in their hands and provide auxiliary contingents to the Roman Army. The Romans then turned against the Sarmatians and gained some important successes over them on the plains of Pannonia. The Sarmatians agreed to sign a peace treaty with Rome in AD 175, according to which they were to contribute 8,000 soldiers to the Roman Army. Some 5,500 of these were sent to Britain, where they garrisoned the northern border and protected it from incursions by Celtic raiders from Scotland.

Germanic warriors preparing an ambush. (*Photo and copyright by Ancient Thrace*)

Germanic warrior equipped with club and round shield; note the horn, which was used to communicate. (*Photo and copyright by Ancient Thrace*)

Before Marcus Aurelius could consolidate the Roman military presence north of the Danube, an internal revolt (headed by the usurper Gaius Avidius Cassius) broke out in the eastern provinces and prevented the emperor from expanding the Roman territories along the northern *limes*. In AD 177, the Marcomanni and the Quadi revolted and attacked the Roman garrisons that were stationed on their territories. The Marcomanni were easily crushed by Marcus Aurelius, but military operations against the Quadi took longer to bring to a successful conclusion. Marcus Aurelius died in AD 180 while the campaign against the Germani was still going on, although the Romans had already prevailed in two pitched battles. Marcus Aurelius' son and successor, Commodus, had little interest in continuing the campaigns against the Germani and in stabilizing the northern frontiers of the Empire. Consequently, he concluded a superficial peace treaty with the Marcomanni and the Quadi without solving the problems of the Danubian *limes*. By the end of the bloody Marcomannic Wars, which had tested the military resources of Rome to their limit, a total of sixteen legions were permanently stationed on territory that bordered with Germanic lands. It is interesting to note that during the Marcomannic Wars, the first communities of Germani were permitted to settle inside the borders of the Roman Empire: these were known as *laeti* and consisted of defeated 'barbarians' who received land in exchange for military service in the Roman Army. The Antonine Plague had depopulated large areas of the Empire, severely reducing the recruiting potential of Rome, so Marcus Aurelius started this early 'experiment' to boost the size of the useful population. It was not a great success: the defeated Germanic warriors soon rose up in revolt, and even briefly seized the major city of Ravenna (one of Rome's main naval bases). The agreement granting land to a community of *laeti* might specify a once-and-for-all contribution of recruits or a fixed number of recruits required each year. The lands given to Germanic settlers were known as *terrae laeticae* and were not part of the normal provincial administration, since they were under the direct control of a specific administrative officer known as the *Praefectus Laetorum*. In addition to the Germani, a good number of Sarmatians were also settled in Italy and Gaul as military colonists.

Chapter 7

The Migration Period and the Battle of Adrianople

Around AD 200, a few decades after the end of the Marcomannic Wars, several 'new' Germanic tribes appeared on the borders of the Roman Empire. These were all migrating from Eastern Europe and, after having settled in eastern Germania, were starting to exert an increasing pressure on the Germanic communities that had always lived in western Germania. Several of the new Germanic groups coming into contact with the Romans were not 'tribes' in the classical sense of the term; they were conglomerations of tribes that comprised many smaller communities. The most important of these was the Alamanni, whose name meant 'all men' and who fought against the Romans for the first time during the reign of Caracalla (AD 213). The Alamanni attacked the Roman frontier in its most exposed area: the *Agri Decumates* (the 'Decumatian Fields'). This was located in present-day south-western Germany and linked up the *limes* of the Rhine with that of the Danube. The Decumatian Fields were the only place of continental Europe where the border of the Roman Empire was not marked by the Rhine or the Danube; as a result, they were particularly exposed to foreign invasions and had been heavily fortified by the Romans. By conquering the Decumatian Fields, an enemy of Rome could easily outflank the defences of the Rhine to the north-west or those of the Danube to the south-east. The Alamanni settled just outside the Roman fortifications of the Decumatian Fields and started to attack them during the early decades of the third century. In AD 235, the emperor Severus Alexander was assassinated by his own soldiers while campaigning against the Alamanni, which led to the beginning of the 'Crisis of the third century', which came very near to causing the fall of the Roman Empire. Since its creation, the Roman state had never experienced such a complex and multi-factorial emergency. All aspects of the Empire's life were affected: political, economic and social. Foreign invasions and internal revolts were key elements of the 'Crisis of the third century', which saw the Alamanni conquering the Decumatian Fields in AD 260 and the secession of all the western provinces of the Empire. These provinces, comprising Iberia and Gaul in addition to Britain, proclaimed their independence from Rome as the 'Gallic Empire' and started to fight in an autonomous way against the Germani.

Germanic warrior with full personal equipment; the planks of the unpainted shield are clearly visible. (*Photo and copyright by Ancient Thrace*)

Germanic chieftain with spear and hexagonal shield. (*Photo and copyright by Ancient Thrace*)

In such a situation, characterized by enormous political chaos, other Germanic 'conglomerations' appeared on the borders of the Roman state. These included that of the Franks, who settled on the eastern bank of the Rhine and had as their main objective the invasion of Gaul. The Roman military situation in the West remained extremely difficult even when the secession of the Gallic Empire was crushed, due to the presence of the Alamanni and the Franks. In the eastern provinces, meanwhile, the relative stability of the early third century was soon endangered by the arrival of the most powerful of all the Germanic conglomerations: that of the Goths. The most numerous of the eastern Germani, the Goths had lived for a long time in the plains of modern Poland and Ukraine (not far from the River Volga). However, coming under strong pressure from the warlike peoples of central Asia, they now wanted to cross the Danube and establish their new homeland south of the great river. Initially, the Roman authorities tried to find a compromise with the Goths, paying them in exchange for providing military contingents to serve in the Roman Army. This was the beginning of a process that would see the progressive 'barbarization' of the Roman Army, which started to comprise an increasing number of Germanic soldiers whose loyalty towards Rome was very unstable and who were commanded by their own officers. For numerous reasons, including the diffusion of the new Christian religion, the Roman manpower available for the military forces of the Empire was decreasing very rapidly. As a result, the imperial authorities had no choice but to employ an increasing number of barbarians to fill the gaps among their troops. These Germanic soldiers could be recruited as single mercenaries (*bucellarii*) or as warriors who were part of an allied community (*foederati*). Sometimes, in exchange for their military services, the *foederati* were permitted to settle inside the borders of the Empire in order to act as farmer-soldiers. This new system, however, soon revealed its limits and produced an increasing fragmentation of Roman territory.

In AD 250, the Goths, together with the Carpi and other Germanic groups, broke the Roman defences on the Danube and invaded the Balkan provinces of the Empire. The Germani successfully besieged Philippopolis and then defeated a large Roman military force at the Battle of Abritus. This clash took place south of the Danube and ended in complete disaster for the Romans: Emperor Decius, who was in command of the three legions that tried to stop the Goths, was killed and his army was routed. After this great victory, the Goths returned north of the Danube after signing a peace treaty, the terms of which were humiliating for the Romans: the Germani were permitted to bring with them all the goods that they had plundered in the Balkans, while the Empire was to pay an annual tribute to them in order to preserve its territorial integrity. The bloody campaigns fought between the Romans and the Germani during the third century were completely different from those of the previous age. The Germani were now migrating towards the Empire and thus did not limit themselves to conducting rapid incursions. They had no fear of the Romans and no aversion to confronting them on the open field. In addition, it should be noted that the eastern Germani had some military peculiarities. For example, having been in close contact with the steppe peoples, they had introduced heavy cavalry and archers into their military forces. These two elements had never been a large-scale element of the Germanic armies that had fought the Romans during the previous centuries. With the fall of the Decumatian Fields, the Alamanni and the Franks started to launch frequent raids against the western bank of the Rhine. At the same time, new groups such as the Vandals and the Burgundians appeared along the *limes* in search of new lands. After Diocletian's ascendancy to the throne in AD 284, the Roman Empire was completely reorganized from an administrative point of view and a certain stability was restored. Under Constantine the Great, the Roman Army was reformed, leading to a general improvement in the situation along the borders. The Germanic attacks were successfully repulsed for several decades, but this did not last for long. After Constantine's death in AD 337, the Empire was enveloped by a series of violent civil wars between the heirs of the defunct emperor. These conflicts involved the participation of an increasing number of Germanic warriors, both mercenary and allied.

The basic idea behind Constantine's reform of the Roman Army was to create a new fundamental distinction between military units, with the field armies separated from the border troops. The field armies were garrisoned in the major cities of the Empire, as highly mobile strategic reserves, while the border troops were garrisoned along the *limes*, serving as the first line of defence against foreign attacks. The reform was based on the new principle of defence in depth. In case of simultaneous attacks on various points of the border, the frontier troops were to stop the enemies for just a few hours or days; in the meantime, the field armies would be rapidly assembled and sent against the invaders. This new system had a great advantage: the presence of the field armies in the major cities of the Empire proved very important for the internal security of Roman territories because these elite troops could be used to crush rebellions or secessions. By the time of Constantine, internal stability was as important as defence against foreign invasions. As a result of these new principles, all the military units of the Roman Army were divided into two large categories: the *comitatenses* (field troops) and the *limitanei* (border troops). In many respects, the *comitatenses* were the direct heirs of the former legions, while the *limitanei* had many characteristics in common with the old *auxilia*. The *comitatenses* were all the units that made up a field army, known as a *comitatus*; the *limitanei* were all those units stationed on the border. The former were elite troops with excellent equipment

Germanic warrior armed with scramasax. (*Photo and copyright by Ancient Thrace*)

Germanic warrior with small rectangular shield. (*Photo and copyright by Ancient Thrace*)

and training, mostly legions or cavalry *vexillationes* (detachments); the latter were organized into smaller units with a strong local character, usually showing a high degree of foreign influence (many units of *limitanei* were equipped more or less like their direct enemies). The border troops were obviously much more static than the *comitatenses* and were strongly linked to the defensive positions that they had to protect. They were a mix between border police and garrison militia, being the perfect troops to counter small incursions or for skirmishing activities. Most of the Roman border regions were characterized by an endemic state of low-intensity conflict, something that the *limitanei* were prepared to face on a daily basis.

Generally speaking, the *limitanei* had lighter equipment than the *comitatenses* and enjoyed less privileges (such as tax exemptions) than the field troops; at the end of their service, however, they received some land located near the border that they had defended for most of their lives. Analyzing this important element, it is possible to suppose that Constantine wanted to create a whole new class of soldier-colonists as the *limitanei* would be defenders of the frontiers with a strong personal link to the border lands of the Empire. This view is confirmed by the fact that by the time of Constantine, the profession of soldiering became mostly hereditary, so members of the *limitanei* would have passed their land properties to their sons and thus protection of the borders would be guaranteed by these military families. According to their functions, the *limitanei* could assume special denominations: if they were stationed on the Rhine or Danubian frontiers, they were commonly known as *riparienses* because their tract of frontier was marked by a river; if they were garrisoned in large border forts, they were known as *castellani*; if they were in smaller forts or watchtowers, they were known as *burgarii*. On special occasions, for example during a military emergency or for a major campaign, some units of *limitanei* could be attached to the *comitatenses*. In this case they received the denomination of *pseudocomitatenses*, whose period of service with the field armies was generally quite limited, but on some occasions the best such units could remain attached to the field troops forever.

The *comitatenses* were grouped in several field armies, located across the regions of the Empire. There was, however, a special category of field army: the *comitatus praesentalis*, or 'the army in the imperial presence'. This was the emperor's own field army, which was under his direct control. Each of the other field armies was commanded by a high-ranking officer known as a *magister militum*, who was assisted by a *magister peditum* (commander of the infantry) and *magister equitum* (commander of the cavalry). As time progressed, the *comitatus praesentalis* also started to be commanded by a *magister militum* like all the other field armies. The most senior units of the *comitatenses* field armies were known as *palatini*; they could be legions, cavalry *vexillationes* or *auxilia palatina*. The latter were elite light infantry

Duel between two Germanic warriors. (*Photo and copyright by Ancient Thrace*)

Duel between two Germanic warriors. (*Photo and copyright by Ancient Thrace*)

units created by converting the semi-regular groups of Germanic warriors that served with the Roman Army into proper regular corps. The *auxilia palatina* were generally named after the 'barbarian' tribe from which they had been recruited, although some could be named after the emperor who had raised them. As previously mentioned, the last decades of existence of the Roman Army were characterized by a process that is commonly known as barbarization. Indeed, the armed forces reformed by Constantine eventually started to include an increasing number of irregular military units formed by Germanic warriors. Generally speaking, the foreign irregulars serving within the Roman Army could belong to two different categories: the *bucellarii* (mercenaries) and the *foederati* (allies). After the military defeat at Adrianople against the Goths, many leading Roman military commanders started to expand the forces under their command by recruiting large contingents of Germanic mercenaries. The term *bucellarii* derives from the word *buccellatum*, a type of dry biscuit that was the ordinary ration of the Germanic professional soldiers. These mercenaries enlisted singularly or in groups and were assembled into units that were under the direct orders of their employers. More or less each *magister militum* started to have several units of mercenaries among his forces. These Germanic troops, directly paid by their employer, generally proved to be very loyal towards the various Roman officers but had no allegiance with the emperor or the central administration of the state. In practical terms, it could be said that several 'private armies' had emerged inside the Roman Empire. Over time, the use of *bucellarii* became increasingly common. Many Roman nobles, especially in the provinces, started to assemble security forces made up of Germanic mercenaries. Since the central state was in great difficulty, many rich landowners preferred to use foreign professional soldiers to protect their private properties. Sometimes these private bodyguards could be converted into regular military units, like the *Placidi Valentiniaci felices*, who had been originally recruited as *bucellarii* by the empress Galla Placidia and were later converted into an *auxilia palatina* corps.

During the early history of the Roman Empire, both the legionaries and the auxiliaries were all *voluntarii* (volunteers). Compulsory conscription did exist in the Roman Army, but it was used only rarely. Generally speaking, the practice of conscription, which was known as *dilectus*, was used only in case of military emergencies or during the preparation of major campaigns for which large numbers of additional troops were required. This situation changed completely after the 'Crisis of the third century': by the time of Constantine, the Roman Army relied mainly on compulsion for the recruitment of soldiers. All citizens of the Empire were subject to a regular annual levy that was based on a principle known as *indictio*, which was a sort of land tax assessment. Each landowner living on the territory of the Empire was required to provide a certain number of recruits to the imperial army, this number being defined according to the amount of land tax that was due on each of the landowner's estates. Obviously, this channel of recruitment was strongly contested by the various rich landowners, who preferred to keep their best men on their estates for work or for their private defence. In order to retain their best men, they often sent the less fit or reliable peasants who were at their disposal, or they could cheat the authorities by sending sons of soldiers (who were already obliged to serve since military profession was by now hereditary) or vagabonds (known as *vagi*). Clearly, the principle of the *indictio* could be used only in the countryside. It mostly involved peasant recruits and affected the local power of the various landowners. In the urban centres, this land-based conscription could not be applied. As a result, the contribution of the cities to the defence of the Empire was extremely low during the Late Empire. Landowners were also frequently able to convert the conscription requirements into a cash levy that had a fixed rate per recruit due. This was known as *aureum tironicum*, from the word *tirones* that meant 'recruits'.

The various regions of the Empire contributed in different ways to the formation of the military forces. The traditional recruiting areas of Gaul and the Balkans, for example, continued to provide the bulk of the Roman Army's recruits. During the final decades of the Empire's existence, the traditional height and age requirements were progressively abandoned, with the result that the general quality of the soldiers saw a dramatic decline. After being accepted into the Roman Army, each new recruit was marked on one of his arms with a specific brand in order to discourage desertion, which became an enormous problem during the Late Empire. Each new recruit was also issued with an identification disk that was worn around the neck and was given a certificate of enlistment that was known as a *probatoria*. The best recruits were generally assigned to the *comitatenses*, while those with an inferior level of fitness were sent to the static units of *limitanei*. The standard period of service was twenty years for the *comitatenses* and twenty-four years for the *limitanei*; in this respect, the change from the organization of legionaries and *auxilia* had not been particularly significant. All the difficulties related to recruiting had obvious consequences on the strength of individual units, with the military corps of the Late Empire notably smaller than those of the Early Empire. In addition, there was always a massive disparity between official and actual strengths: units in the field were generally much smaller than their theoretical establishment. *Foederati* troops were recruited from all those tribes that were allied to Rome due to the terms of a treaty, known as a *foedus*. Generally speaking, the allied tribes of the *foederati* were provided with benefits by Rome in exchange for military assistance. Their loyalty towards the Empire, however, was not very stable: most of them, like the Goths or the Franks, later transformed

Germanic warrior playing his horn. (*Photo and copyright by Ancient Thrace*)

Goth warriors. (*Photo and copyright by Ancient Thrace*)

themselves into fully independent 'barbarian nations' living within the Roman borders. On some rare occasions, the military collaboration between Rome and the Germanic allies had positive results, such as when Flavius Aetius defeated Attila's Huns at the Battle of the Catalaunian Plains (see next chapter). On most occasions, however, the Germanic tribes accepted a *foedus* just to enter the Roman Empire and then create their own independent realm. From an organizational point of view, the contingents of *foederati* were commanded by their own leaders and retained their Germanic military traditions.

During the 350s, Emperor Julian campaigned against the Alamanni and the Franks on the Rhine. He was able to crush the Franks in a decisive battle at Strasbourg in AD 357, but he had to accept the presence of some Frankish communities on the territory of the Empire. After the Battle of Strasbourg, Julian was able to restore the Roman defences of the Rhine frontier and even launched several punitive raids against the Germanic tribes. Some of these tribes were forced to become *tributarii* of Rome and thus started to pay an annual tribute. A few years after his success against the Alamanni, however, Julian launched a massive campaign against the Sassanid Persians in the Middle East, which ended in complete failure with Julian's death and the loss of precious military forces that were fundamental for the defence of the Empire. A few years after Julian's death, all the improvements obtained thanks to the Battle of Strasbourg were already lost and Gaul was again plundered by the Germani. In AD 369, the Romans abandoned their province of Dacia, which was extremely difficult to defend since it was located north of the Danube. A few years later, in AD 376, the Goths entered the territories of the Roman Empire in great numbers. By that time the Roman state was already divided in two parts, each of which was ruled by an autonomous emperor: the Western Empire and the Eastern Empire. Being pressed by the Huns, who were moving from the steppes of central Asia, many thousands of Goths camped north of the Danube and asked the local Roman authorities (of the Eastern Empire) for permission to cross the river in order to settle in the Balkans. Valens, at that time the supreme ruler of the Eastern Empire, welcomed the Goths as *foederati* and permitted them to cross the Danube. He intended for the newcomers to act as military colonists and defend the eastern portion of the Danubian *limes* on behalf of Rome. The Goths, however, were treated very badly by the Roman officials who supervised their settlement: they did not receive the promised food and were forced to live in a state of misery.

Consequently, the Goths rebelled against the Romans and started to plunder the provinces south of the Danube in search of new land where they could survive. In AD 378, after some minor and indecisive clashes, Valens marched at the head of his army against the Goths. The Romans built a strong fortified camp near the city

Germanic warrior with full personal equipment. (*Photo and copyright by Ancient Thrace*)

Germanic warriors patrolling in the woods. (*Photo and copyright by Ancient Thrace*)

of Adrianople before moving against the Goths, who were camped not far from the Roman positions. The Germani, led by the expert Fritigern, had their families and their wagons with them since they were migrating across the Balkans. After a difficult march under the sun, the Roman soldiers reached the enemy camp tired and dehydrated. The Goths, meanwhile, formed a defensive circle with their wagons and placed their infantry inside it, with the cavalry operating independently. The Germanic camp was built on top of a hill and was thus a good defensive position. In order to harass the Romans and delay their advance, the Goths set fire to the fields surrounding the hill. The Gothic cavalry was away from the battlefield since it was conducting a foraging expedition; as a result, Fritigern needed to gain some time before the Romans attacked his positions. Then, without receiving any precise order from their commander, the Roman soldiers attacked the Goths in an uncoordinated fashion and were easily repulsed. When it seemed that they could break the Gothic defences, Fritigern's cavalry appeared on the battlefield and charged the attackers. Surrounded, the Romans were completely routed. Valens was killed, together with many of his soldiers. After the Battle of Adrianople, the Goths became a stable presence inside the borders of the Roman Empire, being by now too strong to be defeated. The following decades saw the outbreak of new civil wars inside the Empire, which culminated in the Battle of the Frigidus River in AD 394. This clash was fought between the Western Empire of the usurper Eugenius (who supported pagan polytheism) and the Eastern Empire of Emperor Theodosius I (who supported Christian monotheism). The battle, probably the bloodiest in the history of the Late Empire, included the participation of thousands of Germanic warriors as part of both armies. The Eastern Empire, for example, deployed a contingent of 20,000 Goths, while the Western Empire fielded a significant number of Frankish warriors. The clash took place in modern Slovenia, not far from the border that separated the Western Empire from the Eastern one. It resulted in a decisive victory for Theodosius I and for his Christian faith, since Eugenius was killed and his army was completely destroyed. After the Battle of the Frigidus River, the armies of the Western Empire practically ceased to exist, which opened the way for the subsequent invasions that caused its fall.

Chapter 8

The Sacks of Rome and the
Battle of the Catalaunian Plains

In AD 395, Theodosius I, the victor of the Battle of the Frigidus River, died and the Roman Empire was divided definitively between his two young sons: the eastern portion was given to the older Arcadius and the western portion to the younger Honorius. Following these events, two Germanic warlords assumed indirect control over the Roman state, since both Arcadius and Honorius were too young to rule without a regent: Stilicho in the Western Empire and Alaric in the Eastern Empire. Stilicho was a half-Vandal who had married the niece of Theodosius I and became the regent of Honorius, while Alaric was a Goth who was appointed as *magister militum* by Arcadius. After the Battle of the Frigidus River, and with the subsequent ascendancy of Alaric, the Gothic communities divided themselves into two main groups: the Visigoths or 'Western Goths' and the Ostrogoths or 'Eastern Goths'. The Visigoths, whose first monarch was Alaric, consisted of those Goths who already lived inside the borders of the Roman Empire and had already been partly 'romanized' from a cultural point of view, while the Ostrogoths were those Goths who were now starting to migrate south of the Danube and were still strongly influenced culturally by the steppe peoples. Around AD 400, the Ostrogoths came under increasing pressure from the Huns and started to move in great numbers towards Roman territory, together with several other groups of eastern Germani who were allies or subjects of the Huns. This migratory movement caused the final collapse of the Western Empire, which was already crumbling under attack from other Germanic tribes such as the Alamanni and the Franks. During his early career, Stilicho served with distinction under Theodosius I and rapidly became one of the most important generals of the Roman Army. After participating in the Battle of the Frigidus River, he was appointed by the emperor as the guardian of the young Honorius. Alaric, as overlord of the Goths, also fought at the Frigidus River, where he met Stilicho for the first time. During the following years, the two 'barbarian' generals would fight against each other in a series of violent wars.

After the death of Theodosius, Alaric hoped to become the guardian of Arcadius and to obtain an important political role inside the administration of the Eastern Empire. However, he was prevented from doing so by the ascendancy of Stilicho, so

Germanic tribal warriors. (*Photo and copyright by Ancient Thrace*)

Germanic warrior with scramasax and round shield. (*Photo and copyright by Ancient Thrace*)

decided to invade the Balkans with his warriors. Alaric rapidly advanced south and was able to raid most of Greece without encountering any serious opposition; the Eastern Empire was in a state of complete chaos, with different political factions vying to influence the young Arcadius. In AD 397, seeing that the situation in the east was becoming desperate, Stilicho landed in Greece and defeated the Visigoths in Arcadia. Alaric, however, escaped capture and continued to ravage the Balkans until he was finally appointed *magister militum* by Arcadius. Between AD 398 and 400, Stilicho fought against the Picts in northern Britain and crushed a rebellion in northern Africa. Alaric, meanwhile, started planning his first invasion of Italy. In AD 402, the Visigoths launched their attack but were halted and defeated by Stilicho at the Battle of Pollentia in northern Italy. This was a severe blow for Alaric, since his wife was captured by Stilicho and most of his best warriors were killed. Curiously, the Battle of Pollentia was the last military victory for which a triumph was celebrated in Rome. In AD 405, there was a major invasion of Italy by a coalition of Germanic tribes, which included the Vandals. Stilicho, against all the odds, was able to repulse this attack despite his forces being numerically far inferior. A few months after this victory, however, the great Germanic general received bad news from the frontier of Gaul: a large number of Germani had crossed the Rhine and were devastating Roman territories north of the Alps. While these events took place on the *limes*, the usurper Constantine III revolted in Britain and seceded from the Western Empire. Unable to face the new military situation that was developing, Stilicho lost the support of the Senate and of his military forces. His men mutinied in AD 408 and organized a coup, which was instigated by Stilicho's political rivals and ended with the execution of the half-Vandal general. Following Stilicho's death, Italy descended into chaos, the local population massacring thousands of Germanic women and children from the families of the *foederati* soldiers who operated in Italy. Presenting himself as the defender of the Germani, Alaric invaded Italy for the second time and besieged the city of Rome.

After two years of siege, during which he tried to obtain some significant territorial concessions for his Visigoths from the Senate, Alaric occupied Rome. Hunger was the most powerful 'weapon' of the Germanic warriors besieging the city, since the inhabitants lacked sufficient food reserves and were forced to resort to cannibalism in order to survive. The siege of Rome organized by Alaric was not a permanent one, since it consisted of three separate shorter sieges that took place during a period of two years. The Western Empire no longer had an effective military force that could expel the Visigoths from Italy, and thus the Germanic warriors were completely free to move around the peninsula. In AD 410, Alaric's men finally entered Rome and sacked the city, but despite Roman fears, they did not commit any atrocities and killed no civilians. Just a few buildings were burned, with all the properties of the Church being spared. Alaric still wanted to present himself as a Roman official rather than a cruel 'barbarian' invader. Shortly after conquering Rome, he moved south towards Sicily with the intention of invading North Africa (where the grain needed by Italy was produced). During the crossing of the strait that connects mainland Italy with Sicily, however, the fleet of the Visigoths was battered by a storm. Alaric died a few days after this unlucky event, probably of fever. In AD 423, Emperor Honorius died, having been unable to defend Rome from the invasion of the Visigoths or to preserve the territorial integrity of the Western Empire. His death caused the outbreak of a new civil war inside the Roman world, with a usurper known as Joannes proclaimed emperor in the west while the eastern emperor Theodosius II (son of Arcadius, who had died) appointed his cousin Valentinian as western emperor. This new civil war ended when an expeditionary corps from the east invaded Italy and deposed Joannes, who died in AD 425. As a result, Valentinian became supreme ruler of the west and started to exert his power from Ravenna (the new capital of the Western Empire), together with his ambitious and intelligent mother, Galla Placidia.

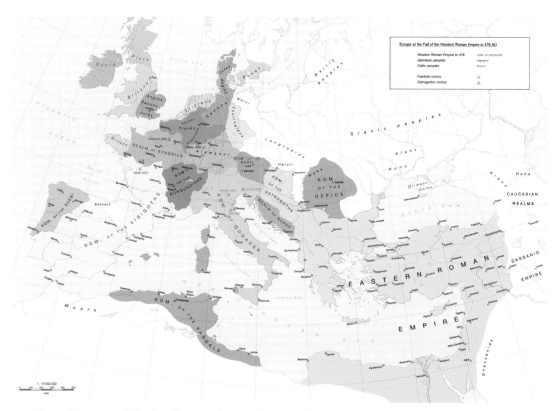

Map of Europe in AD 476, showing the early Romano-Germanic Kingdoms that emerged in the late fifth century. (*CC BY-SA 4.0, Wikimedia User 'Guriezous'*)

Germanic oval shield. (*Photo and copyright by Ancient Thrace*)

During the civil war that ended with the ascendancy of Valentinian, Joannes sent one of his best military officers to the lands of the Huns with orders to raise a large force of Hunnic warriors and return as soon as possible to Italy in order to fight against the soldiers of the Eastern Empire. This officer was Flavius Aetius, an intelligent and capable commander who had spent most of his early life as a hostage at the court of the Hunnic kings. When Aetius returned to Italy with a large force of Hunnic warriors, he learned that the civil war was over and that his overlord, Joannes, had been defeated. He had no choice but to find a compromise with Valentinian. Aetius was appointed *magister militum per Gallias* and thus assumed control over that important portion of the Western Empire. Aetius ruled Gaul as an independent monarch, since Valentinian and Galla Placidia did not have the military resources to protect the frontier of the Rhine. By that time several Germanic tribes had settled permanently in Gaul and the whole region was in a state of complete chaos: the Rhine was no longer a military barrier and the emperors of the west exerted their authority only over the city of Ravenna. Despite all these difficulties, Aetius did his best to assume effective control over Gaul by using his personal military power as well as diplomacy. Soon after assuming overall command of the Roman troops in Gaul, Aetius obtained a series of victories over the Visigoths and the Franks: the former had settled in southern France, while the latter had occupied large portions of territory on the western bank of the Rhine. The Roman general was not able to expel the Germani from Gaul, but confined them in small areas where their movements could be controlled. Between AD 433 and 450, thanks to his victories, Flavius Aetius was the dominant military and political personality of the Western Empire: he was formally appointed as the 'protector' of Valentinian and continued to fight with success against the Germani in Gaul. Aetius defeated the Visigoths again and forced them to form a military alliance with him in exchange for receiving permission to remain in Gaul. In addition, he crushed the Germanic tribe of the Burgundians who had crossed the Rhine some years before and were now forced to settle on a limited portion of territory. By the time of Aetius' victories in Gaul the Romans had already evacuated Britain (in AD 410) and lost any form of control over Iberia (where the Vandals had settled).

Due to his personal relations with some important members of the Hunnic court, Aetius was always able to deploy significant numbers of Hunnic warriors in his military forces. By AD 450, the Huns had created an immense 'multinational' empire that comprised a large portion of central Asia as well as most of Eastern Europe. They had already attacked and defeated the armies of the Eastern Empire and were now ready to invade the rich territories of Gaul. Aetius, thanks to his diplomatic skills, had formed a strong alliance with the Huns, but this vanished when a new monarch emerged among the nomads of the steppes: Attila. Extremely ambitious, Attila wanted to become the supreme ruler of the Western Empire; as a result, he soon started planning an attack against Gaul. The invasion materialized in AD 451, when Attila crossed the Rhine with a large multinational army. The Huns were completely different from both the Romans and the Germani, being incredibly ferocious and having the best cavalry of the time. Armed with composite bows and mounted on small ponies, they seemed to be invincible. The Germani were literally terrorized by the Huns, probably more than the Romans: their eastern tribes had already fought against and been defeated by Attila's warriors during the previous decades. Consequently, when the menace of a Hunnic invasion of Gaul became apparent, Aetius had no great difficulty in forming a Romano-Germanic military coalition to fight against Attila. By that time, the Romans and the Germani had already found some form of equilibrium between them in Gaul, but this risked being destroyed by the Asian newcomers. If the Huns occupied the Western Empire, the Germanic peoples living in Gaul would have been obliged to abandon the new homelands for which they had fought for so many years. Aetius organized a large military alliance that comprised Romans, Visigoths, Salian Franks, Burgundians, Saxons and Alans; the latter were not a Germanic group, but a steppe people who had migrated towards Gaul with the Germani before being submitted by Aetius. The Hunnic Army of Attila was made up of contingents from a large portion of eastern Europe: Ostrogoths, Rugians, Scirii, Thuringians, Ripuarian Franks, Gepids and Heruli.

The decisive clash between the two coalitions took place in AD 451 and is commonly known as the Battle of the Catalaunian Plains. After entering Gaul, the Hunnic army besieged the city of Aurelianum (modern Orleans), but without success. Aetius moved towards the city before the invaders could occupy it, and thus the pivotal battle was fought not far from Orleans. From an ethnic point of view, the Battle of the Catalaunian Plains could be defined as a clash between the western Germani and the eastern Germani. After several hours of harsh fighting, the western Germani prevailed and Flavius Aetius claimed victory over Attila. During the clash, the Visigoths and the Ostrogoths fought against each other with incredible violence, showing that inter-tribal hate was still a fundamental component of the Germanic civilization. The king of the Visigoths, the great warlord Theodoric, was killed by the Ostrogoths during the battle. The direct consequences of the events that took place on the Catalaunian Plains were extremely important for the history of Western Europe: it is only possible to imagine what would have happened if the Huns had occupied Gaul. In AD 452, Attila attacked the Western Empire again and ravaged most of northern Italy before returning to his main base, which was located in Pannonia (modern Hungary). The great Hunnic warlord was assassinated during

Germanic oval shield. (*Photo and copyright by Ancient Thrace*)

Germanic small oval shield. (*Photo and copyright by Ancient Thrace*)

the following year and his immense empire soon crumbled after the outbreak of a bloody civil war which was fought to determine the identity of his successor. With the death of Attila, Emperor Valentinian became increasingly worried about the personal power of Aetius; as a result, he organized a plot against him. In AD 453, the great Roman general was assassinated and the Western Empire lost its last capable military commander. With Aetius' death, it was just a question of time before Rome would be sacked again. Valentinian was killed by one of Aetius' Hunnic bodyguards, and the Empire soon entered into a new and very chaotic political phase. In AD 455, the Vandals, guided by their king, Genseric, landed near Rome and sacked the city. Once again, the sack was not particularly violent, but the Vandals looted as much as possible and the old capital of the Empire was reduced to an impoverished city. In AD 476, the military leader of the Germanic *foederati* stationed in Italy, Odoacer of the Scirii, deposed the last monarch of the Western Empire (the young Romolus Augustulus): the glory of the Roman Empire was over and a new historical phase had begun for Western Europe. Each of the Germanic communities created their own autonomous 'kingdom' during the following decades:

Visigoths: After settling in south-western Gaul, the Visigoths expanded their territories by conquering most of Iberia and expelling the Suebi from the region. Iberia was occupied quite rapidly and only its north-western part remained independent from the Visigoths, continuing to be inhabited by the Suebi. In AD 507, a great battle was fought at Vouillé between the Franks and the Visigoths for possession of southern Gaul. The Franks, under Clovis, emerged victorious and the defeated Visigoths were forced to abandon most of their territories north of the Pyrenees. From AD 552–555, the Visigoths had to repulse an invasion by the Eastern Empire, ordered by Emperor Justinian, which had as its main objective the reconquest of Iberia. In AD 586, the Visigoths defeated the Suebi and annexed their territories, thereby completing the conquest of modern Spain and Portugal. The Visigothic Kingdom of Hiberia was one of Europe's most important 'Romano-Germanic Kingdoms' until being invaded by the Arabs from AD 711–725.

Vandals: Initially, the Vandals settled in Iberia (AD 409), but after just two decades they were defeated by an alliance of the Romans and the Suebi. Being forced to leave their new homeland, they settled in North Africa not far from the site of the ancient city of Carthage (present-day Tunisia). Here, the Vandals learned how to navigate and built a powerful military fleet; they were the only Germanic people to do so in the Mediterranean, and thanks to their warships they exerted a strong influence over the main islands of Italy (Sicily, Sardinia and Corsica). Acting as pirates and

Germanic hexagonal shield. (*Photo and copyright by Ancient Thrace*)

raiders, they captured enormous amounts of gold until being defeated by the Eastern Romans in AD 533–534. Their kingdom was then occupied by Justinian's forces and thus disappeared from history.

Suebi: The Suebi invaded Iberia around AD 410 together with the Vandals. Some years later, they formed an alliance with the Romans and expelled their former allies from modern Spain. With the subsequent arrival of the Visigoths, however, they were confined to a small portion of the Iberian Peninsula (in the north-west, in modern Galicia and northern Portugal). Despite being quite isolated from the rest of Europe, the Suebi repulsed several attacks of the Visigoths until being conquered by them in AD 586.

Franks: Until AD 555, the Franks were divided into two main groups, that of the Salians and the Ripuarians. Despite this, they were able to conquer the entire territory of Gaul thanks to a series of brilliant military campaigns. In AD 486, ten years after the fall of the Western Empire, they defeated the Roman warlord Siagrius, who still controlled a large portion of northern Gaul. Then in AD 496, the Franks crushed the Alamanni at the Battle of Tolbiac and conquered their territory. After this victory, the Frankish king Clovis converted to Christianity and his people soon became the greatest military supporter of the Church of Rome. In AD 507, thanks to their victory at Vouillé, the Franks expelled the Visigoths from Gaul; some years later, in AD 532, the Franks also attacked the Burgundians and rapidly defeated them. With the annexation of Burgundian territory, they obtained control over the entire territory of Gaul and formed the strongest 'Romano-Germanic Kingdom' of Europe.

Alamanni: The Alamanni occupied a large portion of Central Europe that comprised some territories of present-day France, Germany and Switzerland. Defeated by the Franks in AD 496, they rapidly lost their independence. They tried to regain their autonomy by forming an alliance with the Ostrogoths, but this was crushed by the Franks in AD 539.

Burgundians: After being defeated by Flavius Aetius, the Burgundians occupied a portion of Gaul that was centred on the western Alps (north of Italy). They organized a kingdom that flourished for some decades until being annexed by the expanding Franks in AD 532.

Ostrogoths: After Attila's death, the Ostrogoths returned to their home territories on the Danube (the former Roman province of Dacia). In AD 488, however, they

Germanic hexagonal shield. (*Photo and copyright by Ancient Thrace*)

Germanic rectangular shields. (*Photo and copyright by Ancient Thrace*)

were 'invited' to invade Italy by the ruler of the Eastern Empire, Zeno, who wanted to remove Odoacer from the peninsula. Guided by their famous king Theodoric the Great, the Ostrogoths occupied Italy and killed Odoacer in AD 493. During the following decades, the Ostrogothic Kingdom became the most flourishing realm of Europe, since the Ostrogoths were able to develop a very positive relationship with the local Roman population of Italy. The death of Theodoric in AD 526 was followed by a decade of bloody civil wars, which came to an end in AD 535 when the Eastern Empire of Justinian landed an army in Italy. The ensuing conflict between the Eastern Romans and the Ostrogoths, known as the Gothic War, ended only in AD 554 with the definitive fall of the Ostrogothic Kingdom.

Rugians: This tribe was one of the eastern Germanic communities submitted by the Huns and later settled in Noricum (modern Austria). With the fall of the Western Empire, they became allies of Odoacer but later joined the Ostrogoths when the latter invaded Italy. They were rapidly absorbed by the Ostrogoths.

Germanic round shield. (*Photo and copyright by Ancient Thrace*)

Germanic round shield. (*Photo and copyright by Ancient Thrace*)

Scirii: This tribe was another of the eastern Germanic communities submitted by the Huns. After the death of Attila, they founded an independent kingdom in the former Roman province of Pannonia. This realm was destroyed by the Ostrogoths and the few surviving Scirii joined Odoacer. When Odoacer was defeated by the Ostrogoths, the Scirii disappeared from history.

Heruli: After Attila's death, the Heruli freed themselves from Hunnic control and created their own independent kingdom in the present-day Czech Republic. Part of them supported Odoacer in Italy and were subsequently defeated by the Ostrogoths. Later, around AD 508, the realm of the Heruli was conquered and absorbed by the Langobards.

Gepids: After defeating Attila's successors and obtaining their independence, the Gepids organized a vast kingdom centred around the Carpathian Mountains. Defeated by the Ostrogoths in AD 504, they migrated south and settled in the territory of modern Serbia. Here they flourished for several decades, despite being defeated on several occasions by the Langobards, until being conquered by the Avars (a nomadic people of the steppes) in AD 567.

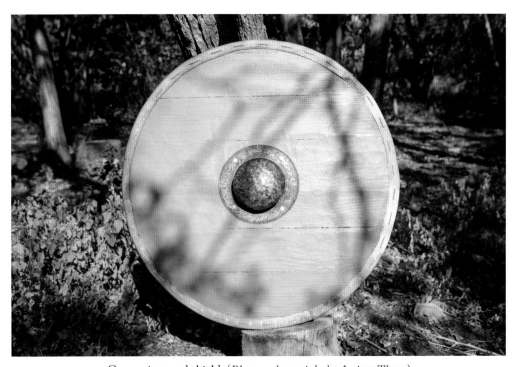

Germanic round shield. (*Photo and copyright by Ancient Thrace*)

Germanic round shield. (*Photo and copyright by Ancient Thrace*)

Back of a Germanic round shield. (*Photo and copyright by Ancient Thrace*)

Saxons: The Saxons, living in present-day southern Denmark, were among the most famous 'piratical peoples' of the Ancient World. Thanks to their great naval skills, they mounted frequent attacks against Britain, raiding it on several occasions before the final withdrawal of the Roman legions from the island. Supported by the Angles, Jutes and Frisians, they became the masters of the English Channel. Around AD 460, the Angles, Jutes and part of the Saxons invaded Britain, where they founded a series of independent kingdoms, which were unified at a later date. The Saxons who remained in continental Europe migrated south and occupied a large portion of north-western Germania. They never organized themselves into a proper kingdom, but continued to retain their tribal social organization as well as their pagan faith. Their territories, collectively known as Old Saxony, remained independent until the ascendancy of Charlemagne and his Frankish Empire. The Saxons resisted foreign invasion for a long time, and were defeated decisively only around AD 800.

Thuringii: Settled in the central part of Germania, the Thuringii remained fully independent until AD 531–532, when they were conquered by the Franks. They later rebelled against the Franks and formed a strong alliance with the Saxons. The Thuringii were permanently submitted by the Franks only during the reign of Charlemagne.

Langobards: Migrating from southern Scandinavia, the Langobards finally settled in present-day Hungary around AD 489. From a chronological point of view, they were the last Germanic tribe to move from its original homeland in search of new lands to

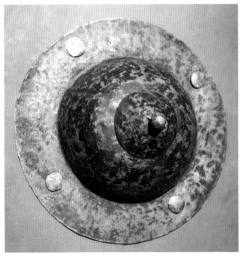

Detail of a round shield's umbo. (*Photo and copyright by Ancient Thrace*)

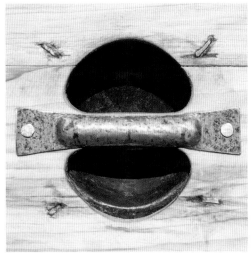

Detail of a round shield's handle. (*Photo and copyright by Ancient Thrace*)

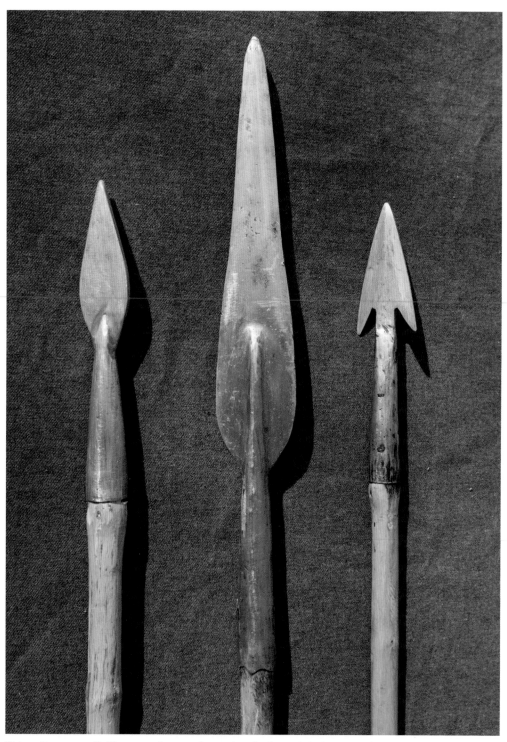

Point of an angon (left), point of a spear (centre) and point of a light javelin (right). (*Photo and copyright by Ancient Thrace*)

Germanic sword and knife with curved blade. (*Photo and copyright by Ancient Thrace*)

Germanic scramasax and short knife. (*Photo and copyright by Ancient Thrace*)

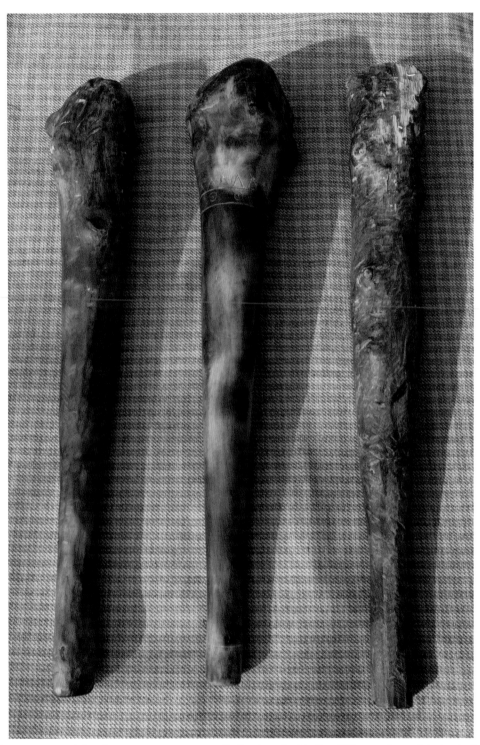

Germanic war clubs; these weapons were usually hardened with fire. (*Photo and copyright by Ancient Thrace*)

Germanic offensive weapons and shields. (*Photo and copyright by Ancient Thrace*)

Germanic offensive weapons and shields. (*Photo and copyright by Ancient Thrace*)

Germanic sling with its stone projectiles. (*Photo and copyright by Ancient Thrace*)

blade to its tip. Butt spikes, also made of iron, were of sockered or tanged fitting. An average Germanic spear was around 2.5 metres long.

In addition to spears, many Germanic warriors also carried a set of light javelins, which were thrown from a distance. These had a shaft that was about 1.1 metres long, thus being much shorter than the spears. Their point was about 13cm in length and had a triangular shape. According to ancient sources, the Germani were masters in throwing their javelins: they could be employed from a great distance and were able to penetrate any kind of armour. Bows were not very common, but a number of warriors in each Germanic army were equipped with them. Their bows were of the type known as *arcubus ligneis*, constructed from a single piece of wood according to the longbow tradition of continental Europe. Historically, peoples living in humid or rainy regions always favoured wooden bows, while those residing in dry or arid regions preferred composite ones. The main advantage of composite bows over wooden longbows was their combination of smaller size and high power. Nevertheless, the Germani employed their simple longbows (which were quite easy to produce) with great accuracy. Swords were used only by the richest Germanic warriors, being seen as a status symbol. During the early phase of the Germani's history, swords were produced according to the contemporary Celtic methods. Their blade had a distinct elongated 'leaf' shape, being double-edged and having a square-kink or shallow 'V' point (the sides of which were drawn at an angle of 45 degrees to the axis of the blade). The tang of these swords (the internal part of the handle, made of metal but covered with organic material) swelled sharply, to a point of greatest width that was placed just below its centre. The ricasso (the unsharpened length of blade just above the handle of the sword) was very short and had a notch that varied greatly in depth. Sword handles were made of wood or leather and generally had the form of an 'X'. The handle was completed by a pommel, which was connected to the tang with a rivet-hole. The blade generally measured about 90cm in length and was entirely made of iron or steel. Germanic swords were used for slashing and not for thrusting; as a result, their blades had a broad neck, with the greatest width being usually low down towards the point. They were transported in iron scabbards, richly decorated with incisions and/or bosses. Scabbards reproduced the general shape of the blade and were constructed from two plates: the front one, slightly wider than the back plate, was folded over the latter along the sides. Scabbards were generally suspended on the right hip from a sword belt made of leather. Knives and short daggers, frequently having curved points, were carried by most of the Germanic warriors. They were used as weapons but also as working tools. Instead of the spear, many Germani used the axe as their main weapon. This was an extremely versatile weapon as it could be used in close-combat but could also be easily thrown. Germanic war axes from this period

Germanic clothes. (*Photo and copyright by Ancient Thrace*)

Germanic fibula, used to hold the cloak in position on the shoulders. (*Photo and copyright by Ancient Thrace*)

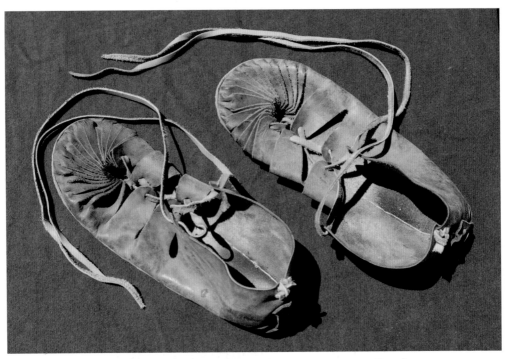

Germanic leather shoes. (*Photo and copyright by Ancient Thrace*)

had an arch-shaped head that widened towards the cutting edge and terminated in a prominent point on both the upper and lower corners.

The general appearance of a Germanic warrior from their early period was very simple. During hot months, only trousers and leather shoes were worn, with most of the men going bare-chested; during winter months, a simple tunic was used, together with a woollen cloak. The cloaks of the richest warriors were held in position by brooches made of precious metal (*fibulae*), which could be decorated in many different ways and have variable dimensions. Garments made of fur, such as waistcoats and cloaks, were extremely popular during cold months. Sleeveless tunics were also produced for warmer months; during winter, these were worn over the long-sleeved ones in order to provide additional protection against the cold. The Germanic trousers, which were soon copied and adopted by the Romans, could have wrap-around puttee-like bindings. Initially, the belts worn around the waist were extremely simple, although they later became larger and started to be fitted with decorative buckles and loops made of metal. Most of the warriors, especially those of the western tribes, had a distinctive hairstyle known as the 'Suebian knot', which was obtained by combing the hair back and tying it into a knot on the right side of the head. Long hair and long beards were also extremely common, together with another kind of hairstyle that developed at a later date: side-braids, top-knot and the rear of the skull shaved. Germanic horses of this period were tough but small ponies, mostly used to conduct scouting and skirmishing missions. Their harness was rudimentary and comprised just a few metal fittings. The saddle was a folded blanket that was held in position by a leather cinch.

Later, especially during the third century AD, the military equipment of the Germanic warriors started to change in a significant way. The nobles, for example, began equipping themselves with helmets and simple cuirasses made of chainmail. At the same time, new types of offensive weapons were also introduced. Germanic helmets were of a model technically known as *spangenhelm*, a term that is clearly of Germanic origin, since 'spangen' refers to the metal strips that formed the framework of this kind of helmet and 'helm' simply means 'helmet'. The characteristic metal strips of a *spangenhelm* connected three to six steel or bronze plates. These made up a framework that had a conical design, which curved with the shape of the head and culminated in a point. The front of the helmet generally included a nasal, but a *spangenhelm* could also incorporate a section of chainmail for protection of the neck (which formed a sort of aventail). Some surviving examples of this kind of helmet also include a sort of eye-protection with a shape that resembles modern eyeglass frames; a few examples include a full facial mask. Older *spangenhelms* often had cheek-flaps made of metal or leather. In general terms, the *spangenhelm* offered

Nice example of *spangenhelm* helmet. (*Photo and copyright by Contubernium Primum*)

effective protection for the head and was relatively easy to produce. It could have heavy decoration, especially if the helmet belonged to a rich warrior. Many surviving examples have evidence of decorative silvering or are covered by costly silver-gilt sheathing. Helmets of senior warlords could be decorated with several glass gems located on the bowl and the cheekpieces.

Armour could be of the *lorica hamata* or *lorica squamata* type, the first found more commonly among the western Germani and the other being popular with the eastern Germani. The *lorica hamata*, or chainmail, comprised alternating rows of closed washer-like rings punched from iron sheets and rows of riveted rings made from drawn wire that ran horizontally, which produced very flexible, reliable and strong armour. Each ring had an inner diameter of about 5mm and an outer diameter of about 7mm. Up to 30,000 rings would have gone into one *lorica hamata*, and the estimated production time for this type of cuirass was two months. Although labour-intensive to manufacture, this kind of armour, with good maintenance, could be used by a warrior for several decades. The *lorica hamata* usually covered the legs as far as the knees; its sleeves could be long or short. The *lorica squamata*, or scale armour, was made up of small metal scales sewn to a fabric backing. The individual scales (*squamae*) could be of iron or bronze. The metal was generally not very thick, commonly being 0.5–0.8mm. Since the scales overlapped in every direction, however, the multiple layers gave good protection. Scales could have rounded, pointed or flat bottoms with the corners clipped off at an angle. They could be flat, slightly domed or have a raised midrib/edge. The scales were wired or laced together in horizontal rows that were then laced or sewn to the backing. Each scale therefore had between four and twelve holes: two or more at each side for wiring to the next scale in the row, one or two at the top for fastening to the backing, and sometimes one or two at the bottom to secure the scales to the backing or to each other. Sometimes the *squamae* could be tinned. Initially, both the helmets and the cuirasses were used only by the richest warriors, but over time the great majority of the Germanic warriors started to be equipped with these defensive elements. The eastern Germani, in particular, were heavily influenced by the steppe peoples living on their borders, and thus developed bodies of heavy cavalry within their military forces. These were made up of cataphracts who wore scale armour and were armed with a specific model of cavalry lance, the contus.

The contus was about 4 metres long and had to be wielded with two hands while controlling the horse using the knees, which made it a specialist weapon that required a lot of training and good horsemanship to use. Initially, only highly trained cavalrymen, such as those fielded by the Sarmatians, could use this lance in an effective way. The contus was reputedly a weapon of great power, especially compared to other

Detail of the cheek-pieces of a *spangenhelm* helmet. (*Photo and copyright by Contubernium Primum*)

Germanic warriors in Roman service, equipped with *lorica hamata*; the figure on the left has a *spangenhelm* helmet and seax short sabre. (*Photo and copyright by Cohors Prima Gallica*)

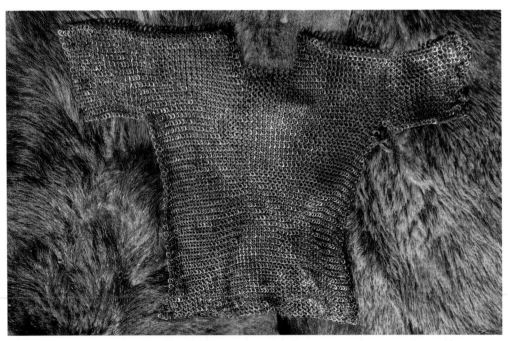

Example of a *lorica hamata* corselet with short sleeves. (*Photo and copyright by Jomsborg Vikings Hird*)

Example of a *lorica squamata* corselet without sleeves. (*Photo and copyright by Jyrki Halme*)

cavalry spears of its time. The great length of this lance was probably the origin of its name, since the Greek word *kontus* means 'oar' or 'barge-pole'. The Roman cavalry adopted the contus on a large scale, like the Germani, after facing the Sarmatian heavy cavalry in battle. Apparently, the eastern Germani also adopted the composite bow of the steppe peoples' light cavalry, albeit on a smaller scale. This bow was made from horn, wood and sinew laminated together. The horn was on the inside facing the archer, while sinew was on the outer side of the wooden core. This gave the bow its shape and dimensional stability. When the bow was drawn, the sinew (stretched on the outside) and horn (compressed on the inside) stored more energy than did wood for the same length of bow. The construction of a composite bow was a very complex process, requiring more varieties of material than a wooden bow and much more time. The composite bow was often made of multiple pieces joined together with animal glue in V-shaped splices. Pieced construction allowed the use of woods with different mechanical properties for the bending and non-bending sections: the wood of the bending part of the limb had to endure intense shearing stress. A thin layer of horn was glued onto what would be the belly of the bow, which could store more energy than wood in compression. Goat and sheep horn was commonly used for this purpose. The sinew, soaked in animal glue, was then laid in layers on the back of the bow, with the strands of sinew orientated along the length of the bow. The sinew was normally obtained from the lower legs and back of wild deer or domestic hooved animals. Sinew would extend farther than wood, again allowing more energy storage. Hide glue was used to attach layers of sinew to the back of the bow and to attach the horn belly to the wooden core. Almost all composite bows were recurved, since this design gave higher draw-weight in the early stages of the archer's draw.

During the period of the Great Migrations, three new offensive weapons were added to the traditional panoply of the Germanic warriors: the angon, the seax and the francisca. The angon was a heavy javelin with a barbed head and a long narrow socket or shank, which was made of iron and mounted on a wooden shaft. The barbs of the head were designed to lodge in enemy shields so that it could not be removed. The long iron shank prevented the head from being cut from the shaft. The angon was likely designed, like the Roman pilum, to disable enemy shields and thus leave enemy combatants vulnerable. The shaft could be decorated, and sometimes iron or bronze rings were fitted onto it to mark the centre of balance and thus the best place to hold the weapon. The seax (also known as a scramasax) was a short sword, mostly but not exclusively used by the cavalry, that came into use among the eastern Germani and was later adopted by a great number of Germanic warriors. Its name meant 'knife' in the Germanic language, and the term 'Saxon' is apparently derived from it. This short sword had a large and single-edged blade, which had a tang in

Germanic warlord equipped with *spangenhelm* and lamellar cuirass. (*Photo and copyright by Confraternita del Leone/Antichi Popoli*)

Germanic warlord from the time of the Great Migrations; note the mail aventail attached to the back of the helmet. (*Photo and copyright by Confraternita del Leone/Antichi Popoli*)

the centreline that was inserted into an organic hilt made of wood or horn. The seax was worn horizontally inside a scabbard made of leather, which was attached to the waistbelt of each warrior (inside the scabbard, the edge of the blade was upwards). Sometimes a small side-knife, with its leather scabbard, was attached on the front of the short sword's scabbard. The francisca, like the seax, first came into use among the eastern Germani, but later became the 'national' weapon of the Franks. Apparently, the Franks' name gave birth to the term francisca. It was a light axe, mostly designed to be thrown from a distance. It had an arch-shaped head, which widened towards the cutting edge and terminated in a prominent point at both the upper and lower corners. The top of the head was S-shaped or convex, with the lower portion curving inward and forming an elbow with the short wooden haft. According to ancient sources, the Germani threw their light axes with incredible accuracy, so the francisca was particularly feared by their opponents.

The shields and swords of the Germanic warriors also changed considerably during the time of the Great Migrations. A new model of oval or round shield came into use, which was either dished (bowl-shaped) or flat. The oval/round shield was much larger than those used previously and was constructed in a different way, being made of solid planks instead of plywood and supported by a double grip (at the elbow and hand). The new shield was typically about 110cm high and 90cm wide, being constructed with 1cm-thick wood planks, and covered and bound with leather. In addition, differently from the previous models, it had a reinforcement made of metal on the external edge and could be decorated with many bronze or iron fittings on the external surface. A hollow iron or bronze boss covered the central hand grip. The new sword, similar to the contemporary Roman spatha, had a straight and long blade. The standard length of the blade was between 0.75 metres and 1 metre, making this a slashing sword. Pommels could be richly decorated and had a distinctive shape consisting of two interlocking rings, which probably symbolized the oaths of loyalty binding a warrior to his overlord.

The military tactics of the Germani changed together with the equipment that they used in battle. At the beginning of the period taken into account in this book, the main tactical formation of the Germanic peoples was the 'boar's head' or *cuneus*: this had the shape of an equilateral triangle, with the commander of the formation being at the apex. The best warriors were deployed near the apex, while those with little combat experience were placed at the rear of the formation. The *cuneus* was employed by the infantry as well as the cavalry. Over time, the warriors in the front ranks started to be equipped with helmets and cuirasses, while those at the back of the *cuneus* were mostly armed with throwing weapons. The chosen warriors of the first ranks followed the movements of their commander very closely, and were in turn followed by the fighters of the other ranks; as a result, the *cuneus* could move very rapidly and was extremely flexible. If stopped by enemy resistance during an attack, the triangular *cuneus* rapidly turned into a more solid rectangle, with the warriors of the rear ranks advancing to support those who were near the apex of the formation. If the *cuneus* was the main offensive formation of the Germani, the shield wall was their

Germanic warrior armed with angon heavy javelin and francisca throwing axe. (*Drawing by Benedetto Esposito*)

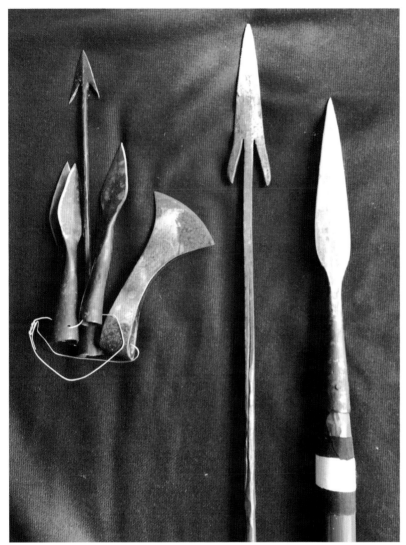

Points/blades of different Germanic weapons (from left to right): light javelins, francisca axe, angon heavy javelin and spear. (*Photo and copyright by Jyrki Halme*)

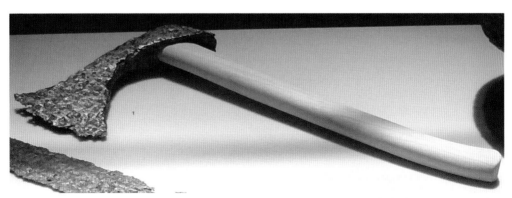

Blade of an original francisca axe, mounted on a reconstructed wooden shaft. (*Author's collection*)

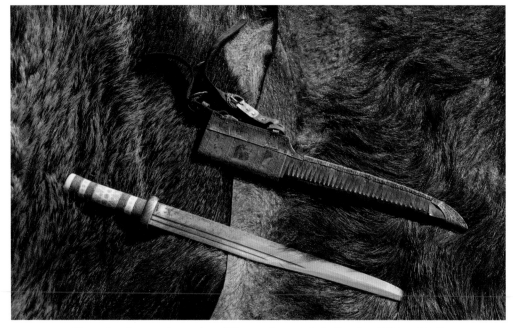

Example of a seax short sabre. (*Photo and copyright by Jomsborg Vikings Hird*)

main defensive formation. This consisted of a large rectangle formed by warriors who were compressed shoulder to shoulder, with their shields overlapping in order to form a 'wall of wood'. When fighting on the defensive, the Germanic cavalrymen usually dismounted and deployed to form a shield wall. This tactic was particularly effective, as shown by the events of the Battle of the Catalaunian Fields, during which the Germani repulsed several Hunnic cavalry charges.

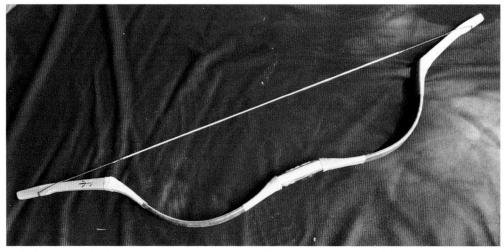

Composite bow, of the same kind employed by the eastern Germanic tribes during the Great Migrations. (*Photo and copyright by Jyrki Halme*)

Bibliography

Primary sources
Ammianus Marcellinus, *Res Gestae*
Appian, *Roman History*
Claudian, *De Bello Gothico*
Claudian, *De Consulatu Stilichonis*
Diodorus Siculus, *History*
Dionysios of Halikarnassos, *Roman Antiquities*
Eusebius of Caesarea, *Chronicon*
Eusebius of Caesarea, *Historia Ecclesiastica*
Livy, *History of Rome from its foundation*
Philostorgius, *Historia Ecclesiastica*
Plutarch, *Lives*
Polybius, *The Histories*
Priscus of Panium, *Historia*
Quintus Aurelius Symmachus, *Relationes*
Socrates of Constantinople, *Historia Ecclesiastica*
Sozomen, *Historia Ecclesiastica*
Strabo, *Geography*
Theodoret, *Historia Ecclesiastica*
Tyrannius Rufinus, *Historia Ecclesiastica*
Zosimus, *Historia Nova*

Secondary sources
Baker, P., *Armies and Enemies of Imperial Rome* (Wargames Research Group, 1981).
Bishop, M.C. & Coulston, J.C., *Roman Military Equipment From the Punic Wars to the Fall of Rome (Oxbow Books, 2006).*
Brzezinski, R. & Mielczarek, M., *The Sarmatians 600 BC–AD 450* (Osprey Publishing, 2002).
Connolly, P., *Greece and Rome at War* (Frontline Books, 1981).
Cowan, R. & McBride, A., *Imperial Roman Legionary AD 161–284* (Osprey Publishing, 2003).
Cowan, R. & O'Brogain, S., *Roman Legionary AD 284–337* (Osprey Publishing, 2014).
D'Amato, R. & Sumner, G., *Roman Military Clothing (3): AD 400–640* (Osprey Publishing, 2005).
Elliot, P., *Legions in Crisis: Transformation of the Roman Soldier AD 192–284* (Fonthill Media, 2014).
Elton, H., *Warfare in Roman Europe AD 350–425* (Clarendon Press, 1998).
Esposito, G., *The Late Roman Army (Winged Hussar Publishing, 2016).*
Goldsworthy, A., *The Fall of the West: The Slow Death of the Roman Superpower (*Weidenfeld & Nicolson, 2009).

Gorelik, K., *Warriors of Eurasia* (Montvert Publishing, 1995).

Luttwak, E., *The Grand Strategy of the Roman Empire* (Johns Hopkins University Press, 1976).

Macdowall, S. & Embleton, G., *Late Roman infantryman 236–565 AD* (Osprey Publishing, 1994).

Macdowall, S. & Hook, C., *Late Roman cavalryman 236–565 AD* (Osprey Publishing, 1995).

Macdowall, S. & McBride, A., *Germanic Warrior AD 236–568* (Osprey Publishing, 1996).

Nicasie, M., *Twilight of Empire: The Roman Army from the Reign of Diocletian until the Battle of Adrianople (Brill Academic Publishers, 1998).*

Nicolle, D. & McBride, A., *Romano-Byzantine Armies 4th–9th centuries* (Osprey Publishing, 1992).

Quesada Sanz, F., *Armas de Grecia y Roma* (La Esfera, 2014).

Sumner, G., *Roman Military Clothing (1): 100 BC–AD 200* (Osprey Publishing, 2002).

Sumner, G., *Roman Military Clothing (2): AD 200–400,* (Osprey Publishing, 2003).

Syvanne, I., *Military History of Late Rome 284–361* (Pen & Sword, 2014).

Syvanne, I., *Military History of Late Rome 361–395* (Pen & Sword, 2015).

Treadgold, W., *Byzantium and Its Army, 284–1081* (Stanford University Press, 1995).

Warry, J., *Warfare in the Classical World* (Salamander Books, 1997).

Wilcox, P. & Embleton, G., *Rome's Enemies 1: Germanics and Dacians* (Osprey Publishing, 1982).

The Re-enactors who Contributed to this Book

Ancient Thrace

The living history association Ancient Thrace was created in 2015 as a group of historical re-enactment by enthusiasts from Yambol in Bulgaria, who were fascinated by the ancient history of their land and wanted to express their passion for it. The group now has around twenty regular members and many 'friends' from different places who often join in with its activities. The efforts of our group has as its main aim that of reconstructing the lifestyle, culture and military equipment of the Thracian tribes in the period between 400 BC and AD 100. As the years passed by, we also started to reconstruct other peoples living in the Balkans during Antiquity: Celts (300 BC–AD 100), Germani (AD 100–200) and Goths (AD 300–400). In our activities and reconstructions we try to be as historically accurate as we can. Our equipment is based on countless hours of interpreting ancient documents and archeological evidence; our process of research and experimentation never stops. During recent years, we have participated with success in several festivals in Bulgaria and abroad; we have also collaborated in the creation of movies and books. All these positive experiences have increased our confidence and stimulated the general improvement of our group. Since we created Ancient Thrace, we have visited amazing destinations and met great people, learned more about history and shared great memories together. For us, historical re-enactment is a special passion that combines our interest in history with our desire to learn more about the past. We wish to reach people and share with them the emotions of this passion, which has become a very important component of our daily life.

Contacts:
Facebook: https://www.facebook.com/AncientThrace/

Index

Agrippa, 77
Ahenobarbus, 70
Alesia, 54
Angrivarii, 95
Aquae Sextie, 30–1
Arausio, 21–2, 26–7, 36
Ariovistus, 40, 42–4, 47, 50, 56
Armorica, 43

Bordeaux, 21
Bronze and Copper Road, 4
Bructeri, 78
Bucellarii, 111, 117

Caetrati, 59
Carnutum, 104
Chatti, 64, 66, 78, 94–5, 101, 104
Chauci, 64, 73, 78, 95, 101, 104
Cisalpine Gaul, 37, 40
Cohortes equitate, 56
Commodus, 107
Crassus, 37

Decumatian Fields, 108, 112
Drusus, 63–4, 66–7, 76

Eburones, 51

Frigidus, 124, 125
Fritigern, 124

Gaius Julius Civilis, 98
Galba, 63
Galla Placidia, 117, 129, 131
Gergovia, 51
Gnaeus Papirius Carbo, 18, 21
Great Bog, 84

Hannibal, 14, 21–2, 24, 26, 59

Jastorf culture, 5, 7, 8

Kalkriese, 81, 84

Longhouse, 4

Macedonia, 11, 17–18
Magetobriga, 40, 44, 47
Maroboduus, 74, 90–1, 95–6, 101
Marsi, 78, 95
Mauri, 54, 59

Nero, 63–4, 94, 98
Nordic Bronze Age, 1, 4, 7
Noricum, 17–18, 21, 104, 139
Numidians, 54, 59

Perseus, 11
Philip V, 11, 17
Philippopolis, 111
Pompey, 37, 59

Ravenna, 107, 129, 131

Sabis, 43
Segestes, 81
Senate, 18, 21, 22, 37, 40, 44, 60, 128
Sicambri, 63, 67, 78
Spartacus, 37
Strasbourg, 121
Suetonius, 87

Tigurini, 21
Tirones, 118
Transalpine Gaul, 37, 40

Usipetes, 63, 64

Valentinian, 129, 131, 135
Vercellae, 31, 36
Vesontio, 42, 47, 50
Voluntarii, 117
Vosges, 50

Weser, 64, 81, 95